IMAGES
of America

NEWHALL'S WALK OF WESTERN STARS

Coauthor Kim Stephens stands at the start of Newhall's Walk of Western Stars across from the entrance to William S. Hart Park. The walk has had different names over the years, including the Western Walk of Fame and the Western Walk of Stars (as seen here), before settling on its current moniker. (Photograph by E.J. Stephens.)

On the Cover: Robert Taylor, Bill Hart, and Gal, one of Hart's harlequin Great Danes, sit in front of the grave of Hart's famous pinto pony, Fritz. Walk of Western Stars inductees are currently honored every year during the Santa Clarita Cowboy Festival, which is based at William S. Hart Park in Newhall, where one can visit Fritz's grave. (Courtesy of SCVhistory.com.)

IMAGES
of America

NEWHALL'S WALK OF WESTERN STARS

Bill West, E.J. Stephens,
and Kim Stephens

ISBN 978-1-4671-0621-4

Published by Arcadia Publishing
Charleston, South Carolina

Printed in the United States of America

Library of Congress Control Number: 2020944378

For all general information, please contact Arcadia Publishing:
Telephone 843-853-2070
Fax 843-853-0044
E-mail sales@arcadiapublishing.com
For customer service and orders:
Toll-Free 1-888-313-2665

Visit us on the Internet at www.arcadiapublishing.com

Dedicated to all the great honorees who gave us the magic of the West, to their fans who gave them stardom, and to the countless elected officials and volunteers who saw fit to give them their saddles.

Contents

ACKNOWLEDGMENTS

Kim and E.J. would like to thank E.J. and Kim for being each other's partner and co-conspirator in all things. They also send lots of love to their two-legged youngins, Mariah and Dylan; to their four-legged ones, Hank and Stella; and to their friends and families—especially to their parents, Pherbia Stephens and Dick de Geus, who are still vibrant and causing trouble as they enter their 90s. They would also like to thank their buddy Bill West, who did a lot of the heavy lifting on this book, and for providing most of the yucks on *SCV In The Movies*.

Bill thanks (and appreciates, loves, and adores) his wife, Liliana, and their son Josh for supporting him and holding down the fort while he disappeared for long stretches of time to work on this book. Bill is indebted to Kim and E.J. for offering to include him on this, one of their many books. These guys are real professional writers, and Bill couldn't be happier to be along for the ride!

The authors wish to thank Leon Worden, a man who wears many hats in the Santa Clarita Valley. Leon is the president of SCVTV, the manager of SCVnews.com, the pooh-bah of SCVhistory.com, and the executive producer of *SCV In The Movies*. Leon also serves on a few boards around town during his spare time. Many of the images contained in this work came from SCVhistory.com via the Jo Anne Darcy Collection, Santa Clarita Valley Historical Society archive, which Leon maintains. Without Leon and his staff and the assistance of Eva Gritz, this book would not have been possible.

The authors would also like to tip their Stetsons to Friends of Hart Park (FOHP) president Laurene Weste and director Jeff Wheat for their advice and continued support. Thanks also go out to Andree Walper, who was instrumental in reviving the walk after a seven-year hiatus, and to Phil Lantis, David Knutson, Kyle Lopez, Patrick Downing, Jeff Barber, and their teams with the City of Santa Clarita, who bring us the Santa Clarita Cowboy Festival (cowboyfestival.org) every year (pandemic years excluded) and were instrumental in bringing our inaugural Newhallywood Silent Film Festival to fruition in 2020. We look forward to working with you on many more film festivals in the future—can anyone say WOWSfest?

All images are courtesy of SCVhistory.com unless otherwise indicated.

Introduction

The Los Angeles basin is sprinkled with walks of fame. For example, along the sidewalks of Ventura Boulevard in Studio City, you can find a walk of fame honoring productions filmed on the studio lot that was once the home of Republic Pictures. In Westchester, near LAX, you can find a walk of fame dedicated to famous aviators. The city of Burbank has one for famous showbiz animals. Everyone knows about Hollywood's famous Walk of Fame, which is one of Southern California's premier tourist attractions. But fewer tourists—or residents, for that matter—would be able to locate some of Tinseltown's other famous walks, like the Rockwalk, a walk of fame dedicated to rock 'n' roll musicians, or the nearby walk dedicated to porn stars or, believe it or not, the walk on LaBrea Avenue that is there to honor actors who appeared on the 1970s television series *Sanford and Son*.

Another gem hiding in plain sight can be found 30 miles to the north of Hollywood in the quaint section of the city of Santa Clarita known as Newhall. It is here, along a few downtown streets, where you can find Newhall's Walk of Western Stars (WOWS). Inlaid in the sidewalks are bronze saddles surrounded by terrazzo tile squares that honor nearly 100 (and counting) legends of Western film, television, radio, and music who contributed to America's Western heritage since 1900.

Some have asked, "How did a walk of Western stars come about, and why did it find a home in Newhall?" The answer to the second part of the question is simple—Newhall is and was the Old West. Every event the mind conjures up when thinking about that exciting time happened in and around Newhall. It was here, long before there was a city of Santa Clarita, that we had the explorers, cowboys, Native Americans, range wars, shootouts, bandits, floods, trains, train robberies, stagecoaches, dam breaks, rodeos, water wars, gold rushes, earthquakes, missions, land barons, cattle drives, rustlers, and oil booms and busts. The dust had hardly settled on this colorful era before Hollywood filmmakers began showing up, this time to recreate the drama from a few years earlier for a worldwide audience. With all its diverse landscapes and its proximity to Los Angeles, Newhall quickly became one of the world's premier Western filming locations. From the earliest days of the Silent Era, film crews had become a frequent site in downtown Newhall, as well as in other spots around the area, like the man-made slit in the mountains south of town called Beale's Cut and nearby Vasquez Rocks. Newhall was ranch country, and some of the locals began renting their properties out to the studios. The studios soon found it cheaper to own their own spreads and built several filming ranches around town. This was especially true in Placerita Canyon, where Monogram had its ranch, and the Walt Disney Company would later create Golden Oak, its film ranch, on parcels cobbled together from previous studio properties. The old Monogram Ranch would relocate a couple of miles up the canyon and be used for hundreds of Western film productions. Cowboy singing superstar Gene Autry, who had filmed early in his career at the ranch, put it on his bucket list to own the place one day, and his goal was achieved in the early 1950s. The ranch, which Autry renamed Melody Ranch, was the site of thousands of hours of Western filming, creating dozens of the careers that are now honored on the Newhall Walk of Western Stars a couple of miles away. To fill television's insatiable need for Western programming in the 1950s and 1960s, Autry regularly rented the property out to producers and filmed several of his own productions on-site. It was here that Marshal Matt Dillon first stared down the bad guys in *Gunsmoke*.

But it wasn't just film and television producers who found Newhall. Lots of the cowboy heroes who came here to film liked what they saw, and decided to stay. Legendary nickelodeon cowboy hero William S. Hart, one of the Silent Era's biggest stars, came to Newhall after finishing his screen career, building his retirement home on a hill that now overlooks the walk. Harry Carey Sr., John Wayne's friend and idol, lived on a ranch in San Francisquito Canyon with his actress wife, Olive, and their son Harry "Dobe" Carey Jr. Tom Mix created one of his permanent sets, known as "Mixvilles," in downtown Newhall, and his saddle on the Walk of Western Stars can be found in front of one of the remaining Mixville buildings. B-Western star Hoot Gibson was a local, and for a time owned the rodeo grounds that are today used for the Saugus Swap Meet. So, Newhall was the perfect, logical choice for a Walk of Western Stars.

As for the first part of the question, "How did the Walk of Western Stars come about?" we have to go back to the mid-1970s when Jo Anne Darcy, who was head of the local chamber of commerce, came up with the idea of honoring some of these Western film and television stars in a series of meals known as the Western Celebrities Luncheons. Darcy and the chamber later transformed the event into the physical Walk of Western Fame on Main Street in Old Town Newhall in 1981, but after running afoul of the Hollywood Chamber of Commerce for copyright infringement for the use of the name "Walk of Fame," the name was changed to the Western Walk of Stars for a time before settling into its current name. Inductions were held until 1993, when the devastation caused by the Northridge Earthquake the following January brought things to a halt.

Installations on the Walk resumed in 2000, when Darcy was the mayor of the city of Santa Clarita, which contains Newhall. The walk became part of the annual Santa Clarita Cowboy Poetry Festival, later shortened to the Santa Clarita Cowboy Festival, which takes place every April with a celebratory dinner and a public unveiling of the new saddles. After a nomination process, a committee of city employees selects each years' honorees. For years, the Cowboy Festival was held at Melody Ranch's historic Western Town before moving to its current home at William S. Hart Park, where the southern end of the Walk of Western Stars begins.

Since 1981, nearly one hundred stars have been immortalized on the walk. During that initial year, all three inductees—William S. Hart, Gene Autry, and Tom Mix—were honored posthumously. Since then, many of the honorees have been living at the time of their inductions and have attended the unveiling ceremony. The year 1982 saw the induction of Rex Allen, Tex Ritter, and Eddie Dean, three famous singing cowboys. In 1983, legendary Newhall locals Tex Williams and Andy Jauregui were honored along with singing cowboy superstars Roy Rogers and Dale Evans, beloved *Green Acres* shyster Pat Buttram, and television's Claude Akins. The following year saw screen legend John Wayne and *The Lone Ranger*, Clayton Moore, inducted alongside Western television greats Dennis Weaver, Clint Walker, and Robert Conrad. The years 1985–1986 saw the commemorations for Iron Eyes Cody, Monte Hale, and *The Rifleman*, Chuck Connors. Throughout the remainder of the decade, local legends Harry Carey Sr. and Hoot Gibson were honored with Ben Johnson, Dale Robertson, Doug McClure, and Amanda Blake, who spent six years playing Miss Kitty on *Gunsmoke* at nearby Melody Ranch. Only four classes of honorees were represented in the 1990s, due to the devastating Northridge Earthquake of 1994, which stopped new additions from being added to the walk until 2000. During this decade, several Western film, television, and recording stars and stunt performers had their names added to the walk. These included Jack Palance, Woody Strode, Stuart Whitman, Virginia Mayo, Montie Montana, Jane Russell, Hoyt Axton, George Montgomery, Hugh O'Brian, Denver Pyle, Lee Horsley, Morgan Woodward, and Bruce Boxleitner. Country music pioneer Cliffie Stone, who lived in Newhall, was also added to their ranks.

After a seven-year drought, the year 2000 saw the rebirth of inductions along Old Town Newhall's sidewalks. That year, Peter Brown, Don Edwards, and Richard Farnsworth were enshrined. The following year saw Wilfred Brimley and Herb Jeffries honored, along with Santa Clarita resident Linda Gray and WOWS founder Jo Anne Darcy, who is the first, and only, non-Western performer to be honored on the walk. In 2002, local resident Peggy Stewart was joined by fellow honorees Alex Cord and John Schneider, who became famous in *The Dukes of Hazzard*, which was filmed in the canyons around town. The next year, William "Hopalong Cassidy" Boyd, who lived for a time at Melody Ranch, was inducted along with Bruce Dern, Riders in the Sky, and Buck Taylor. In 2004, Keith Carradine, Melissa Gilbert, Buck Page, and local stunt superstar Loren Janes earned their saddles. Powers Boothe, who for three seasons played Cy Tolliver in *Deadwood*, which was filmed at Melody Ranch, was honored in 2005. So was Graham Greene, Jack Williams, and Saugus native Harry Carey Jr. The remainder of the decade saw the inductions of Joel McCrea, David Carradine, John Saxon, Harry Dean Stanton, Sons of the San Joaquin, Rhonda Fleming, Robert Horton, and Andrew Prine. Also honored were locals Jack Lilley and Phil Rawlins, along with James Arness, who spent a great deal of time in Newhall over the years filming *Gunsmoke*. Gary Cooper, James Stewart, Audie Murphy, and Lloyd Bridges formed the class of 2010. Director John Ford was the sole honoree in 2011, and Glenn Ford and Oscar-winning editor and Newhall local Joel Cox were enshrined the following year. In 2013, Lee Marvin was honored along with Stuart Hamblen and Rodolpho Acosta, two men with strong Santa Clarita Valley connections. Charles Bronson and Steve McQueen were enshrined in 2014, and Waddie Mitchell and legendary local stuntman Diamond Farnsworth got their saddles the following year. Another stuntman, Hal Needham, was honored in 2016, along with the amazing Johnny Crawford. The year 2017 saw the enshrinement of our good friends Renaud and Andre Veluzat, and Bo Hopkins was also honored that year. Enshrinements skipped a year in 2018, to return the following year with honorees James Drury, Robert Fuller, and Dan White. Ricky Schroder and the late Cesar Romero were announced as the two honorees for 2020 at the Newhallywood Silent Film Festival in February at William S. Hart Park, but thanks to a tiny little virus that can bring down the toughest of cowboys, their inductions have been put on hold until things can get back to normal.

The final story of Newhall's Walk of Western Stars has yet to be written. There are dozens of current Western stars yet to be honored and lots of space left on the sidewalks of Old Town Newhall to honor them. And thanks to the resurgence of new Westerns coming out of Hollywood, in the future, there will be new stars whose names we currently may not know deserving a permanent home on Newhall's Walk of Western Stars.

The authors of this book contribute to a local television show called *SCV In The Movies* on SCVTV. Oddly enough, the attractive author (Kim) works behind the scenes, but if you can stand looking at Bill and E.J., please check us out on SCVTV if you are in the Santa Clarita area, or online at scvinthemovies.com. You can consider the show a video companion to this book because there you can find interviews with Peggy Stewart, Joel Cox, Clayton Moore's daughter Dawn Moore, Joel McCrea's grandson Wyatt McCrea, Stuart Hamblen's grandson Bill Lindsay, and Mike Fleming, the former director of the Santa Clarita Cowboy Festival, as well as several complete movies featuring our commentary and starring honorees William S. Hart, John Wayne, Clayton Moore, Harry Carey Sr., and Hoot Gibson.

Happy Trails.

Bill West and Kim and E.J. Stephens
Newhall, California, while under lockdown due to Covid-19,
Summer 2020

This map of the Walk of Western Stars in Old Town Newhall shows the locations of plaques along Main Street and a few adjoining streets. William S. Hart Park, in the lower portion of the map, is the home of the Santa Clarita Cowboy Festival. WOWS honorees are awarded their plaques every year during the festival. (Map designed by McGregor Shott, courtesy of the City of Santa Clarita.)

Pictured here are WOWS plaques on the sidewalk in front of Newhall's Canyon Theatre Guild. The plaque in the foreground honors WOWS founder Jo Anne Darcy (see page 66). (Photograph by E.J. Stephens.)

One

The 1980s

In 1981, what was then known as the Western Walk of Fame became a physical reality. That year's inaugural class of inductees were Gene Autry, William S. Hart, and Tom Mix, which is not surprising as each of the three men had extensive ties to Newhall. As a matter of fact, if a couple of rooftops and trees were pushed aside, William S. Hart's retirement home could be seen from his plaque. This is a lobby card from the 1940 film *Melody Ranch*, starring Gene Autry, Jimmy Durante, and Ann Miller. Autry would later rename his movie ranch in Newhall after the film.

BEFORE THE WALK (THE 1970S). What is known today as the Walk of Western of Stars began as a series of luncheons in the mid-1970s called the Western Celebrities Luncheon, which was sponsored by the Newhall-Saugus-Valencia Chamber of Commerce, and hosted by Jo Anne Darcy and Los Angeles County supervisor Michael Antonovich. After the walk became a physical reality, the celebratory lunches became part of the Walk of Western Stars celebration. Above, from left to right, Jane Russell, Jo Anne Darcy, and Stuart Whitman are seen at one of these celebrations. At left are Jane Russell and Michael Antonovich.

Western Celebrities Luncheon (the 1970s). During the Western Celebrities Luncheons in the 1970s, the following Western stars were honored: Tex and Dallas Williams, Jimmy Wakely, Cliffie Stone, Doye O'Dell, Montie Montana Sr. and Jr., Andy Jauregui, Stuart Hamblen, Eddie Dean, Carl Cribbs, Nudie Cohn, Iron Eyes Cody, Harry Carey Jr., Rod Cameron, and Gene Bear. Several of these folks would later get physical monuments on the Walk of Western Stars. Above, Clayton Moore, Moore's daughter Dawn, and Dennis Weaver are pictured at the WOWS celebratory luncheon in 1984. Below, Michael Antonovich and Doug McClure share a laugh at the commemorative lunch for 1988–1989 honorees.

GENE AUTRY (1907–1998), CLASS OF 1981. Of the more than 2,400 performers immortalized with terrazzo and brass stars embedded into the Hollywood Walk of Fame, only singing cowboy superstar Gene Autry has a star in each of the five featured categories of film, television, music, radio, and live performance. Orvon Grover Autry was born in 1907 and grew up on a ranch in Oklahoma. He signed his first recording contract in 1929 and later hosted his own music show on WLS-AM in Chicago, where he met singer-songwriter Smiley Burnette. Hollywood quickly came calling, and Autry headed west to make dozens of enormously successful singing cowboy films over the next 20 years atop his horse Champion, with Burnette often cast as his singing sidekick. Pictured is a lobby card from the 1940 film *Melody Ranch*, which starred Autry, Ann Miller, and Jimmy Durante.

Gene Autry. Gene Autry recorded over 600 songs and sold over 100 million records. He repeatedly struck gold recording Christmas songs like "Santa Claus is Coming to Town," "Here Comes Santa Claus," "Frosty the Snowman," and "Rudolph the Red-Nosed Reindeer." A wise investor, Autry was the longtime owner of Los Angeles's KTLA television station as well as the Los Angeles Angels Major League Baseball team. Melody Ranch in Newhall, another former Autry property, has been seen on screen in hundreds of Westerns, including many made by Autry. He acquired it in 1952 and used it daily for film and television production until August 1962, when a brushfire burned most of it to the ground. For the next three decades, the property served as a retirement home for his horse Champion. Autry passed away at the age of 92 on October 2, 1998, just three months after the death of his friend and screen rival, Roy Rogers. Seen here is a WOWS gathering with, from left to right, Jackie Autry, Chuck Connors, and Gene Autry, with Iron Eyes Cody looking on.

William S. Hart (1864–1946), Class of 1981. Newhall's most famous resident, William Surrey "Two Gun Bill" Hart was born during the Civil War in New York, where he later achieved success as a Shakespearian stage actor. As a boy, Hart traveled throughout the country with his father, interacting firsthand with ranchers, cowboys, and Native Americans. As a witness to the Old West, Hart would later incorporate a more truthful account of this era into his films. At the advanced age of 49, he began his screen career for Thomas Ince's New York Motion Picture Company for $125 per week before moving to Hollywood. His movie career lasted from 1914 to 1925, during which time he was perhaps the most famous actor on the planet. In total, he made 65 films, all silent, which were known for their realism. This is a photograph of the set of a lost Hart film, *The Border Wireless*, from 1918.

William S. Hart. Hart purchased a ranch in Newhall in 1921 and later built a hilltop Spanish colonial–style mansion there called La Loma de los Vientos (Hill of the Winds). The legendary lawmen Wyatt Earp and Bat Masterson and famed Western artist Charles Russell were frequent visitors. During his retirement, Hart turned to writing, penning a dozen novels and his autobiography, *My Life East and West*. He lived with his sister Mary Ellen at the mansion until his death in 1946. He was quoted as saying, "While I was making pictures, the people gave me their nickels, dimes, and quarters. When I am gone, I want them to have my home." A man of his word, as a final act of philanthropy, Hart willed his 265-acre ranch to the people of Los Angeles County to be used as a public park. Seen here is the entrance to Hart Park on Newhall Avenue.

Tom Mix (1880–1940), Class of 1981. Once the biggest film star in the world, former nickelodeon cowboy Tom Mix died on October 12, 1940, when the car he was driving plunged into a washed-out gully south of Florence, Arizona, and his sturdy aluminum suitcase struck him on the head, crushing his skull. Mix claimed to be a child of the West, a former Texas ranger and US marshal, and to have been one of Teddy Roosevelt's "Rough Riders" in the Spanish-American War. In truth, Mix was born in 1880 in Pennsylvania, and though he did sign up to go to war, he remained stateside and never saw combat. He did serve as a lawman in Oklahoma and Kansas but never in Texas. However, unlike many Western film stars, Mix was an expert on a horse and with a gun.

Tom Mix. Fame came quickly to Mix after he made his first film in 1910. By the 1920s, he was making $7,500 a week and oversaw the construction of several Western film sets called "Mixvilles" around Southern California, including one in downtown Newhall. Mix's film career ended with the coming of talkies, but he continued performing on radio on the *Tom Mix Ralston Straight Shooters* program. It is estimated that Mix made over $6 million during his film career (which translates to roughly $400 million today) but spent most of it on high living and costly divorces (he was married five times). He was not quite penniless at the time of his crash, but it may have been better for him if he had been because the suitcase that killed him was filled with money, traveler's checks, and jewels. Seen here is a building that was once part of a Mixville film set. Mix's WOWS saddle can be seen in the sidewalk in front.

Rex Allen (1920–1999), Class of 1982. Rex Allen was born in 1920 on a ranch outside the town of Willcox, Arizona. Teamed with his horse Koko and sidekicks Buddy Ebsen and Slim Pickens, Allen appeared in a series of Westerns, including the last singing cowboy film in 1954. Known as "the Voice of the West," Allen's resonant pipes can be heard in several hit records and in narrations for movies, television shows, cartoons, and theme park attractions for Walt Disney. Below is a lobby card for 1953's *Shadows Of Tombstone*.

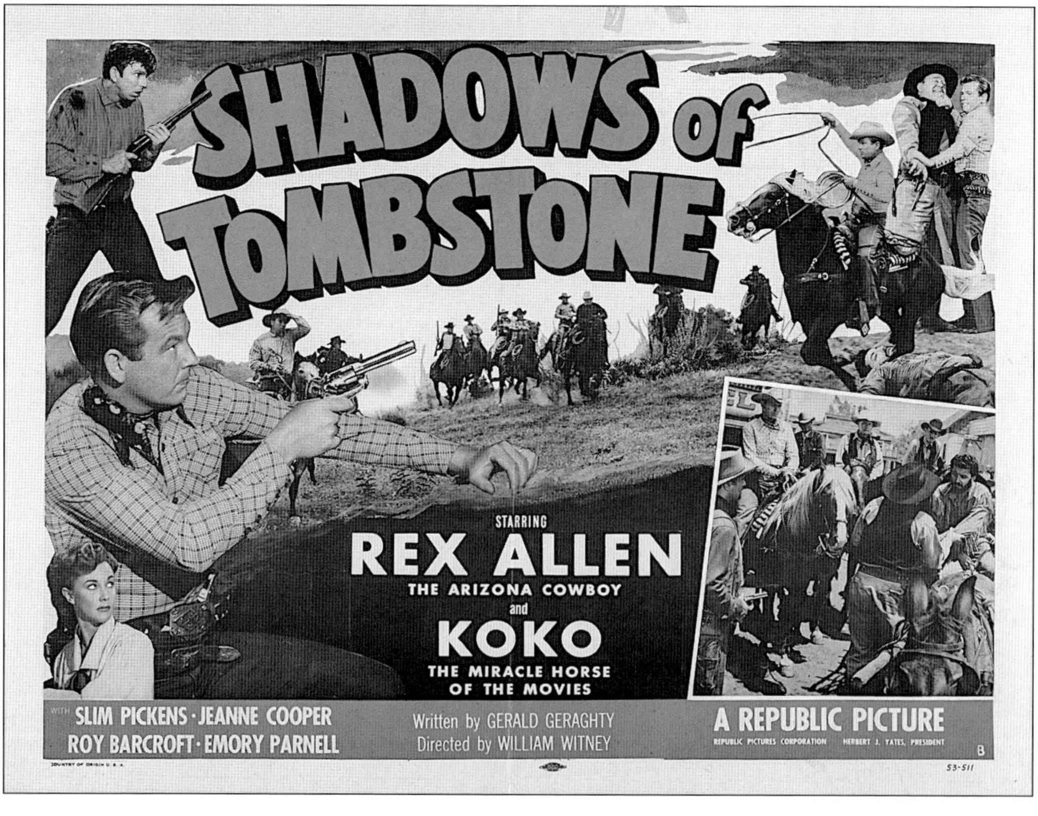

Eddie Dean (1907–1999), Class of 1982. Texas singer Eddie Dean first gained fame alongside his brother on WLS Radio's *National Barn Dance* program in Chicago in the early 1930s. By the middle of the decade, he was appearing in Western films in supporting roles. Both Roy Rogers and Gene Autry believed Dean to be the best cowboy singer of all time. Dean had a hit in 1955 with "I Dreamed of a Hillbilly Heaven," which later became an even bigger hit for Tex Ritter (see page 22). Dean was married to his wife, Dearest, for 69 years from 1930 until his death. Below is a lobby card for 1946's *Tumbleweed Trail*, which starred Dean.

Tex Ritter (1905–1974), Class of 1982. Country Music Hall of Famer Woodward Maurice "Tex" Ritter nearly became a lawyer instead of a renowned singer and Western film star. After graduating with honors from high school in his native Texas, Ritter attended the University of Texas in Austin and Northwestern Law School near Chicago. Luckily for fans of singing cowboy flicks, Ritter was more interested in show business than jurisprudence. After a stint on Broadway, he headed west in 1936 to star in Westerns for Grand National Pictures. Around 40 singing cowboy films later, Ritter went to Universal, where he teamed up with Johnny Mack Brown in a series of films shot during World War II. Ritter had a few more starring roles with Poverty Row studio PRC (Producers Releasing Corporation) but spent most of the remainder of his career as a recording star. In 1952, Ritter's recording of "Do Not Forsake Me Oh My Darlin'," the title track for the film *High Noon*, won the Academy Award for Best Song. Ritter's son John was a popular television star before his untimely death in 2003. This is a still from *Trouble in Texas* (1937) with Ritter and Rita Hayworth.

Claude Akins (1926–1994), Class of 1983. A popular face during a 40-year television, film, and stage career, Claude Akins made his screen debut in *From Here to Eternity*, and appeared in *The Caine Mutiny*, *Rio Bravo*, and *Inherit the Wind* during the 1950s. Akins enjoyed steady work on television Westerns in shows like *Death Valley Days*, *Boots and Saddles*, *The Restless Gun*, *Wagon Train*, *Bonanza*, *The Big Valley*, *Rawhide*, and *Gunsmoke*. One of his best-remembered roles was as Sheriff Elroy P. Lobo in the 1979 series *B.J. and the Bear* and in its spinoff, *The Misadventures of Sheriff Lobo*. Below is a still from *Yellowstone Kelly* (1959) with, from left to right, Akins, Clint Walker, and Edd Byrnes.

Pat Buttram (1915–1994), Class of 1983. Alabama native Pat Buttram began his Hollywood career as a sidekick to WOWS neighbors Roy Rogers and Gene Autry. He was often seen on television in *The Gene Autry Show* (which was occasionally filmed at Autry's Melody Ranch in Newhall) and heard on the radio on Autry's program *Melody Ranch* (which, ironically, was not made at Melody Ranch). His distinctive voice, which he claimed "never quite made it through puberty," can be heard in several Walt Disney animated features in the 1960s. But to millions of fans worldwide, Buttram will forever be Mr. Haney, the slimy salesman from the popular American sitcom *Green Acres* (1965–1971). Below is a publicity shot of the cast of *Green Acres* with Buttram at far left.

Dale Evans (1912–2001), Class of 1983. Born Frances Octavia Smith, "Queen of the West" Dale Evans was a singer and actress who met her future husband, Roy Rogers, on a film set in 1944. Evans appeared in many movies with Rogers, but sometimes received third billing after Rogers's horse Trigger. Rogers and Evans were married over 50 years until Rogers's death and had several children. Evans was a songwriter and wrote Rogers's theme song "Happy Trails" and the spiritual "The Bible Tells Me So." She also wrote religious books and made frequent personal appearances to share her spiritual journey with others. Evans passed away in 2001, three years after Rogers. Seen here are Evans and Rogers at the unveiling of Dale's saddle.

Andy Jauregui (1903–1990), Class of 1983. Longtime Newhall resident and Cowboy Hall of Famer Andy Jauregui (pronounced Ha-REGG-ee) was raised in a family of 13 children on a sheep ranch in Santa Paula. Riding broncos by age 16, Jauregui was soon doubling on horseback for Hollywood stars like Richard Dix in *Cimarron*. During the 1930s, he won world championships on the rodeo circuit in steer roping, calf roping, and team roping and later became a successful rodeo promoter. Jauregui lived on a ranch in Placerita Canyon for over 60 years, which was often rented out for Western productions. For a time, he was in partnership with his neighbor Clarence "Fat" Jones furnishing livestock and equipment to the filmmakers. (One of Jones's daughters later married fellow WOWS honoree Ben Johnson.) Jauregui's ranch later became part of Walt Disney's Golden Oak Ranch, which is used for filming to this day. Jauregui was famous for his generosity and his phrase, "Let's get with it, boys!" which friend and neighbor Harry Carey liked so much he used it in one of his films. Pictured is Jauregui (left) with his friend and neighbor Bill Hart.

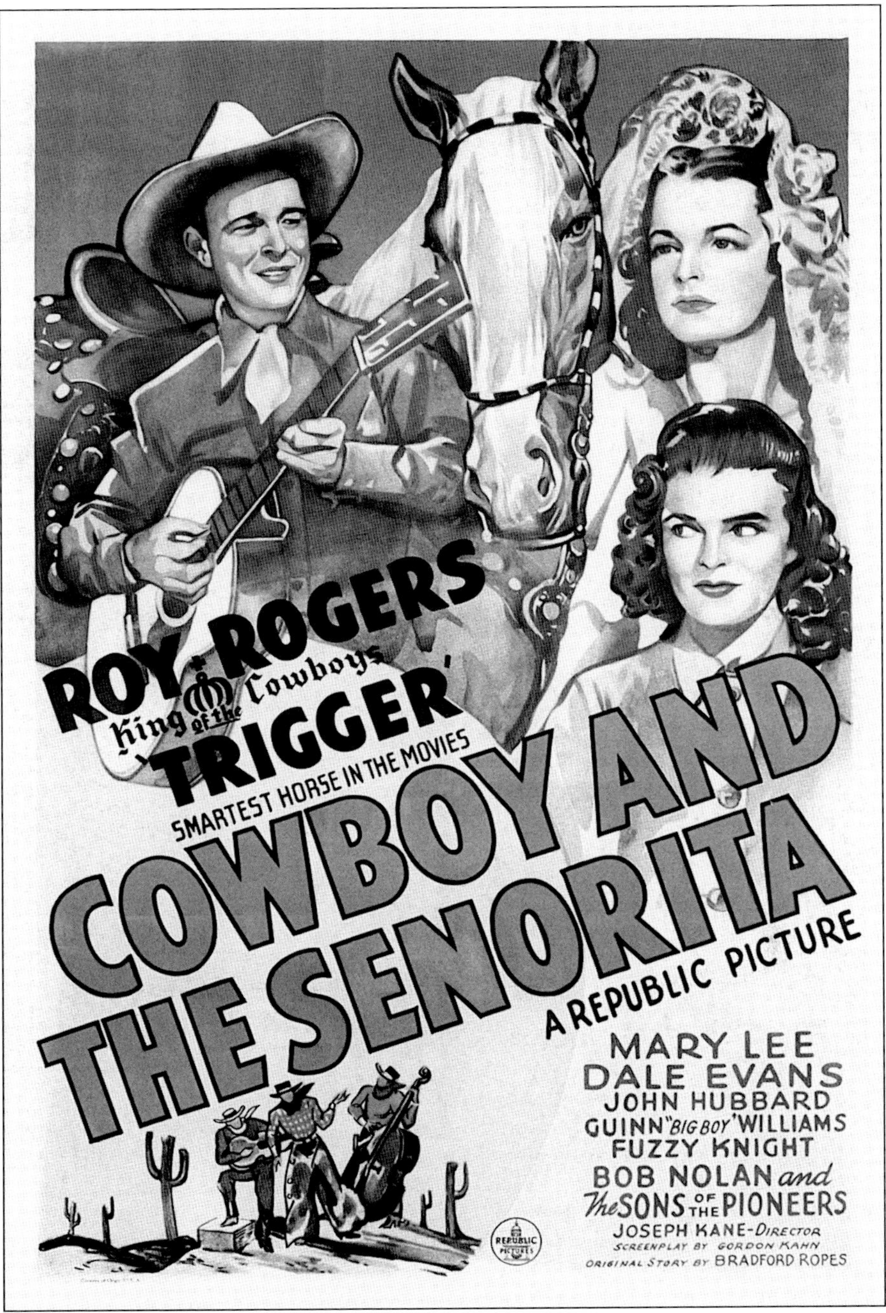

Roy Rogers (1911–1998), Class of 1983. For most of his 100 starring roles on screen, Roy Rogers played . . . Roy Rogers. Hollywood's "King of the Cowboys" was born Leonard Franklin Slye. He first gained fame as a singer fronting the group the Sons of the Pioneers, who had several Western hits, including "Cool Water" and "Tumbling Tumbleweeds." An idol to millions of kids across America, Rogers not only appeared in theaters, but also on television, radio, and of course, lunch boxes. Rogers is one of the few performers to have three stars on the Hollywood Walk of Fame. His ability to masterfully combine the skills of acting and singing has placed him on the Mount Rushmore of "Singing Cowboys." Seen here is the poster for 1944's *The Cowboy and the Senorita.*

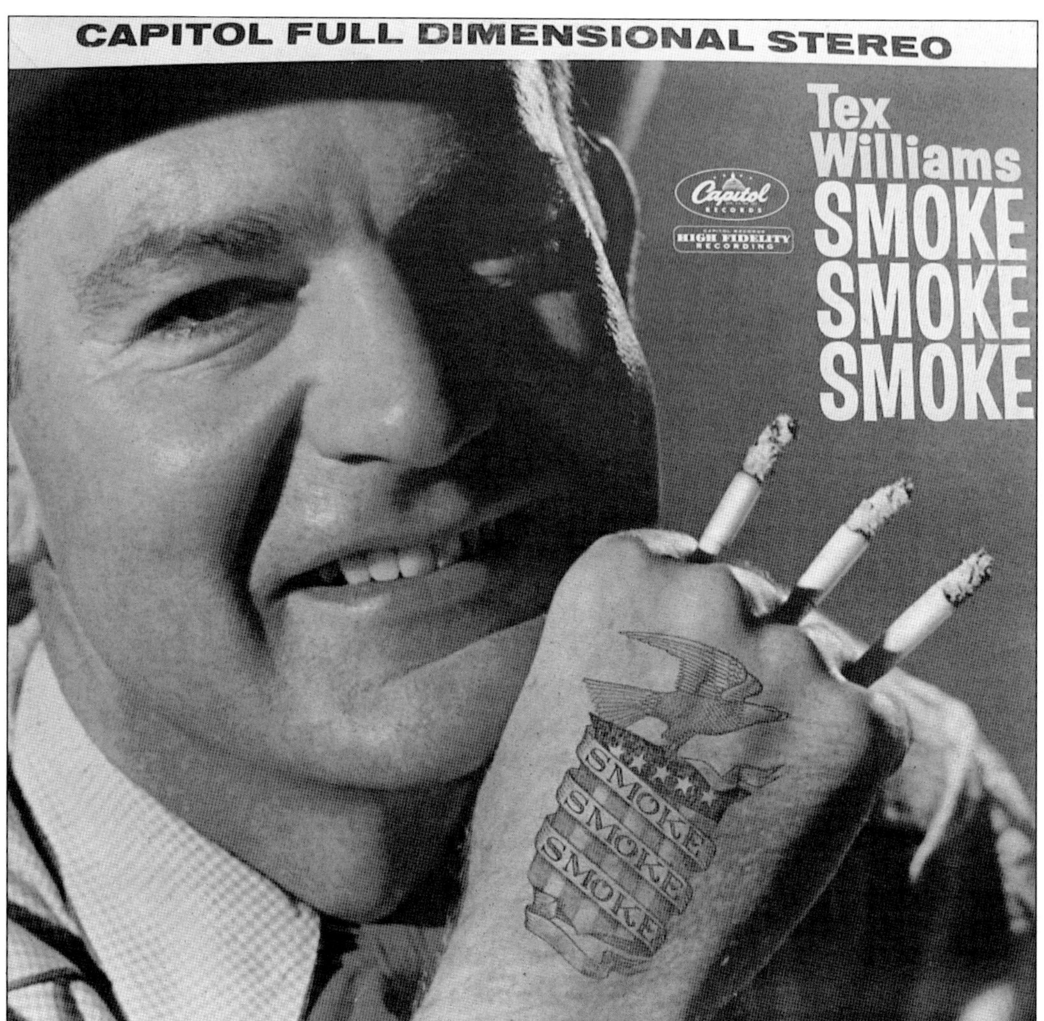

Tex Williams (1917–1985), Class of 1983. Country singer-songwriter and longtime Newhall resident Sollie "Tex" Williams moved to Los Angeles from his home in Illinois after high school and earned his first film role in a 1943 Joe E. Brown movie. During the 1940s and 1950s, he starred in a series of low-budget Western musicals for Universal, known as "oaters." Williams struck musical gold in 1945 as the lead singer of the Spade Cooley Orchestra with the single "Shame on You," which stayed on the country charts for 31 weeks. Newhall neighbor Cliffie Stone later offered Williams his own recording contract, and Tex left Cooley to form Tex Williams and His Western Caravan. In 1947, his single "Smoke! Smoke! Smoke! (That Cigarette)" topped both the country and pop charts, becoming Capitol Records' first million-selling record.

Robert Conrad (1935–2020), Class of 1984. Robert Conrad's career began in 1957 when he met actor Nick Adams while visiting the grave of James Dean in Fairmount, Indiana. Adams, seeing star potential in Conrad, talked him into heading west to seek his fortune in Hollywood. Within two years, Conrad, who was born Conrad Robert Falk in Chicago, had his first starring role as detective Tom Lopaka in *Hawaiian Eye*, a spinoff of the series *77 Sunset Strip*. In 1965, he began his four-year run as the iconic Old West secret service agent James West ("James Bond on horseback") in *The Wild Wild West*, alongside Ross Martin, who played his disguise-wearing, explosive-mixing partner Artemous Gordon. The show was still extremely popular when it was canceled in 1969 due to pressure from Congress to limit television violence. Conrad was back in action in the 1970s as aviator Pappy Boyington in the series *Baa Baa Black Sheep* and pitched Eveready Batteries in often-parodied commercials. Conrad liked to perform his own stunts and was inducted into the Hollywood Stuntmen's Hall of Fame. He died of heart failure in 2020, less than a month before his 85th birthday. This is a publicity photo from *The Wild Wild West*, with Conrad (right) and Ross Martin.

CLAYTON MOORE (1914–1999), CLASS OF 1984. It is hard to imagine Clayton Moore without picturing him in his Lone Ranger mask. But folks may not remember he played over 50 roles for 15 years before he landed the part that would define his career. More surprising still, many of those early roles were as bad guys. Twice, for example, he portrayed Jesse James. He appeared in many movie serials in his early days, including 1949's *The Ghost of Zorro*. A natural athlete, Moore began his career as a circus performer who did a trapeze act at the 1934 Chicago World's Fair. He then became a model and later a stuntman before getting speaking roles. But it was the 10 years that he played "the Masked Man," with his "faithful Indian companion Tonto" (played by Jay Silverheels) and his horse Silver, that made him unforgettable to Western fans everywhere. Moore is pictured at the unveiling of his saddle in 1984.

Clayton Moore. *The Lone Ranger* was the first Western produced specifically for television. Although Moore played the title character in television and movies for only 10 years, he spent an additional three decades making appearances as the Masked Man, including welcoming guests to Frontierland at Disneyland. Though the part of the Lone Ranger has been played by several other actors, it will forever be Clayton Moore associated with the role. Moore reportedly loved playing the character and enjoyed meeting fans of the show. He would never go out of character in front of audiences, wanting them to feel they had met the real Lone Ranger in person. This practice created a special bond between Moore and the Lone Ranger. That connection is perhaps best captured on the Hollywood Walk of Fame, where his star is the only one that lists both the actor and his character. It reads "Clayton Moore—The Lone Ranger." This is a publicity shot of Moore with his horse, Silver.

Clint Walker (1927–2018), Class of 1984. For seven seasons, Clint Walker played Cheyenne Bodie in the first hour-long television Western series, *Cheyenne*. Before securing this breakout role, Walker held several non-acting jobs, such as carnival roustabout, sheet metal fabricator, nightclub bouncer, golf caddy, and oil field worker. While working as a security guard in Las Vegas, actor Van Johnson introduced him to a casting agent. That meeting led to an interview with Cecile B. DeMille to try out for a small role in *The Ten* Commandments. On the way to the interview, Clint stopped to help a woman fix a flat tire. This made him late for the meeting, but it turned out the woman was DeMille's secretary, so his tardiness ultimately won him the role. His barrel-chested good looks and soft-spoken, understated acting style earned him several roles after *Cheyenne*, including that of convict Samson Posey in *The Dirty Dozen*. In 1971, Walker suffered a fall from a ski lift, resulting in being impaled through the chest with a ski pole. First thought to have died, he was saved by emergency surgery, went back to work, and lived another 47 years.

John Wayne (1907–1979), Class of 1984. Marion Morrison acquired his nickname "Duke" (named after the family dog) back when he played football for Glendale High School. It was Wayne's University of Southern California football coach who gave game tickets to Tom Mix through Morrison, who, in return, hired Morrison as a prop boy and extra. From this humble start began one of the most storied film careers in Hollywood history. Morrison, now known as John Wayne, had his big break in John Ford's 1939 Western classic *Stagecoach*, which featured Newhall's historic Beale's Cut. From then on, Wayne was a star and Ford was his favorite director. Besides *Stagecoach*, the duo worked together in *Fort Apache*, *She Wore a Yellow Ribbon*, *They Were Expendable*, *3 Godfathers*, *The Quiet Man*, *The Man who Shot Liberty Valance*, and perhaps most famously, *The Searchers*. In addition to his Walk of Western Stars plaque, Wayne also received an Academy Award and a Congressional Gold Medal and was posthumously awarded the Presidential Medal of Freedom. He remains a hero to millions of Western film fans to this day. Seen here is a publicity photo from 1930's *The Big Trail*.

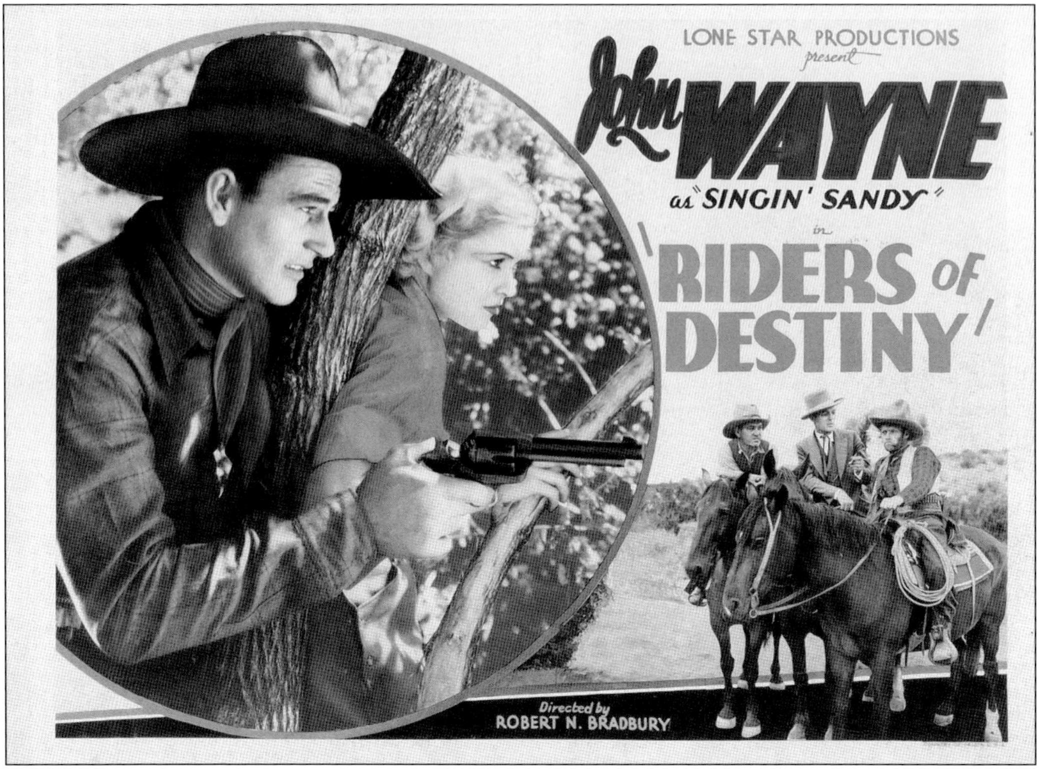

John Wayne. What may surprise many is that John Wayne was among the first "singing cowboys." Long before Roy Rogers, Gene Autry, and Tex Ritter, Wayne portrayed "Singin' Sandy" in 1933's *Riders of Destiny*, which was shot in the Santa Clarita Valley, with some scenes amongst the rubble from the St. Francis Dam disaster, which occurred just a few years earlier. The film was directed by Robert N. Bradbury, whose son also became a famous Western actor with the stage name Bob Steele. Steele knew Wayne from Glendale High School and recommended him to his father. Because Wayne could not sing, Bradbury's other son Bill provided his singing voice. Above is a lobby card from 1933's *Riders of Destiny*. Below is a still from a Singin' Sandy film.

Dennis Weaver (1924–2006), Class of 1984. Dennis Weaver wanted to be an actor from an early age. He committed fully to the profession after failing to make the 1948 US Olympic decathlon team. His acting career was secured in 1955 when he landed the role of Chester, Matt Dillon's deputy, in the long-running Western series *Gunsmoke* (which was filmed for its first six seasons at Newhall's Melody Ranch). Weaver was often seen on television throughout the rest of his career, including starring roles in *Gentle Ben* and *McCloud*. He also starred in the Steven Spielberg thriller *Duel* in 1971, which was also filmed in the Santa Clarita Valley. Weaver was an advocate for the environment and a supporter of several progressive causes. He and his wife, Gerry, had one of the most successful marriages in Hollywood history, lasting from 1945 until his death. Weaver died from lung cancer on February 24, 2006, the same day as Don Knotts, another actor who played a famous TV deputy. This is a still from *Gunsmoke*, with Weaver (right) and Milburn Stone.

IRON EYES CODY (1904–1999), CLASS OF 1985–1986. For years, Iron Eyes Cody was America's most famous Native American. Cody began acting in the early 1930s and appeared in Westerns for his entire career, both on screen and on television, performing alongside some of the biggest cowboy stars of the day, like John Wayne in *The Big Trail*. Cody acted in over 200 films, but it was his appearance as a Native American shedding a lone tear in a 1970s environmental public service announcement that gave him lasting fame. Cody claimed to be a member of the Cherokee tribe, but in one of Hollywood's endless ironies, he may not have been a Native American at all. Near the end of his life, it was suggested that Iron Eyes was, in fact, born in Louisiana to Sicilian immigrants—a claim he vehemently denied. Here, Cody is pictured with Roy Rogers.

CHUCK CONNORS (1921–1992), CLASS OF 1985–1986. Sports came naturally to the strapping six-foot-five Kevin "Chuck" Connors, who learned the game of baseball in the shadow of Ebbet's Field, where his beloved Brooklyn Dodgers played. He earned a scholarship to Seton Hall University to play first base but dropped out after two years to become a tank-warfare instructor during World War II. Connors's first taste of professional sports actually came in basketball when he joined the startup Boston Celtics franchise in 1946. He played with the team just long enough to become the first man in professional basketball history to shatter a backboard during the Celtic's very first game. He soon left basketball behind when he was offered a tryout with the Dodgers. He made the team in 1949 but only appeared in one game before being sent down to the minors. He made it back to "the show" in 1951 after being traded to the Chicago Cubs and appeared in 66 games, batting .238 with 2 homers and 18 RBIs. (Amazingly, Connors was also drafted by the Chicago Bears and nearly played professional football as well.) Connors is at his saddle unveiling with, from left to right, unidentified, Johnny Grant, Johnny Crawford, and Iron Eyes Cody.

Chuck Connors. Had Chuck Connors been a better hitter, he may never have made it in Hollywood. In 1952, he was again demoted to the minors; this time to Los Angeles, where he was spotted by a talent scout and signed to play in the Spencer Tracy–Katherine Hepburn film *Pat and Mike.* After Connors received a check for $500 for his work on the film (which was a huge boost in salary over what baseball was paying him), he thought to himself, "Baseball just lost a first baseman." He acted steadily for the next four decades in films like *Old Yeller*, *Flipper*, and *Soylent Green*, and on television in *Branded* and *Roots*. But he will always be best remembered as Lucas McCain in *The Rifleman*, a role he recalled with pride his entire life. This is a publicity shot from *The Rifleman*, with Connors (right) and Johnny Crawford.

MONTE HALE (1919–2009), CLASS OF 1985–1986. Country music and B-Western star Monte Hale (born Samuel Buren Ely) first gained experience singing in his father's church in Oklahoma. Hale signed a seven-year contract in 1944 with Republic Pictures, where he appeared in dozens of B-Westerns. He also starred in a series of comic books. One of his last roles was in *Giant* (1956), where he taught James Dean how to use a lariat. From left to right are Hale, Rocky Lane, and Roy Rogers in *Trail of Robin Hood* (1940).

AMANDA BLAKE (1929–1989), CLASS OF 1987. Beverly Louise Neill, better known as Amanda Blake, was born in 1929 in Buffalo, New York. She appeared in a few films in the early 1950s before beginning her 19-year run as Miss Kitty on *Gunsmoke* in 1955. A major animal activist, Blake ran her own cheetah breeding program. She was known to occasionally bring her lion Kemo onto the *Gunsmoke* set. Pictured is a publicity photo from *Gunsmoke*, with Dennis Weaver (top), Milburn Stone, and Blake.

Harry Carey (1878–1947), Class of 1987. Harry Carey, who is said to have been John Wayne's idol, was one of the earliest stars of Western silent film. Carey's rugged frame and gravelly baritone voice later carried him successfully into the sound era. Carey lived on a large ranch in Saugus (now the Tesoro Adobe Historic Park) with his actress wife, Olive Golden. Their son Harry Carey Jr. appeared with his parents in two films. In the final shot of *The Searchers*, John Wayne holds his right elbow with his left hand, a frequent Carey pose, in tribute to his late friend. Wayne said at the close of the scene that he and Carey's widow, who was also on screen, wept together.

Ben Johnson (1918–1996), Class of 1987. Academy Award winner Ben Johnson began his Hollywood career when he delivered a load of horses from his ranch in Oklahoma to director Howard Hughes on the set of *The Outlaw* in Northern Arizona. Johnson spent several years as a stuntman on Westerns, including riding double for Henry Fonda in *Fort Apache*. Johnson saved three men from serious injury on that production when the horses pulling the wagon they were in stampeded. This earned the thanks of director John Ford, who signed Johnson to a seven-year contract. Over a long career, Johnson appeared in several Western classics, including *She Wore a Yellow Ribbon*, *Rio Grande*, *Shane*, *The Wild Bunch*, and *Chisum*, often displaying his world-class riding skills. In 1971, Johnson won the Oscar for Best Supporting Actor for his portrayal of Sam the Lion in *The Last Picture Show*. Both Johnson and his father were world champion rodeo riders. In 2019, a museum opened in Pawhuska, Oklahoma, that commemorates the riding achievements of the Johnsons and other local rodeo champions. This is a publicity photo of Johnson in 1961's *One-Eyed Jacks*.

Hoot Gibson (1892–1962), Class of 1988–1989. Like his cinematic peer and Santa Clarita Valley neighbor Gene Autry, Edmund Richard "Hoot" Gibson began his working career as a telegraph operator. As a young delivery boy for the Owl Drug Company, Gibson earned his nickname when he became affectionately known as "Hoot Owl," which was later shortened to "Hoot." A love of horses coupled with his superior riding ability made him a world rodeo champion and landed him a job in 1910 as a stunt rider in D.W. Griffith's *Two Brothers*. Gibson soon became a much sought-after silent star at Universal Studios. His homely yet handsome looks and winning smile filled the character gap between the dashing Tom Mix and the austere William S. Hart, appealing to people of all ages, especially women. He successfully weathered the industry's transition from silents to talkies and continued to star in several Universal Westerns. This is a still with Gibson (right) and Charles K. French from *The Bearcat* (1922).

Hoot Gibson. Hoot Gibson made a fortune during the 1920s but saw his film career decline during the Depression. Bad investments and broken marriages ruined him financially. In 1930, he bought a one-third interest in the Baker Ranch and Rodeo in Saugus (today's Saugus Swap Meet) for $250,000, but the bank later foreclosed on the mortgage. Gibson toured for years with various circuses and spent time as a greeter at a Las Vegas casino. He appeared in the occasional film until 1959, but by the early 1960s, he was dying of cancer. Along with his Walk of Western Stars plaque, Gibson was honored with a star on the Hollywood Walk of Fame and inducted into the Western Performers Hall of Fame. This is a lobby card from 1922's *The Sawdust Trail*, starring Gibson.

DOUG MCCLURE (1935–1995), CLASS OF 1988–1989. In 1962, Southern Californian Doug McClure began his nine-season run on *The Virginian* as the fun-loving, rowdy cowhand Trampas, a role that made him famous. McClure later appeared in several television shows and movies, including *At the Earth's Core*, *The Land that Time Forgot*, and *The People that Time Forgot*, three films based on Edgar Rice Burroughs novels. McClure died of lung cancer at the age of 59. This is a publicity photo from the CBS television series *Checkmate* (1960–1962) with, from top to bottom, McClure, Anthony George, and Sebastian Cabot.

DALE ROBERTSON (1923–2013), CLASS OF 1988–1989. Dale Robertson earned fame from fans of early TV Westerns with his roles as Jim Hardie in *Tales of Wells Fargo*, Ben Calhoun in *Iron Horse*, and as the fourth and final host of *Death Valley Days*. Robertson appeared in over 60 Westerns, and during the final years of his nearly 50-year career, he was cast in shows like *Dynasty*, *Dallas*, and *Murder, She Wrote*. He also hosted a radio show called *Little Known Facts* that was broadcast to over 400 stations. Seen here is a publicity photo of Robertson from *Tales of Wells Fargo* (1957–1961).

Two

The 1990s

The 1990s would see 16 more Western honorees enshrined in the Newhall Walk of Western Stars. A sampling includes performers made famous on screen (Virginia Mayo, Jane Russell, Jack Palance, Woody Strode, and real-life husband and wife Sam Elliott and Katherine Ross), on television (Morgan Woodward, Hugh O'Brian, Denver Pyle), and in western music (Cliffie Stone, Hoyt Axton). In this photograph taken at the 1990 WOWS induction dinner are, from left to right, Morgan Woodward, Hugh O'Brian, and Denver Pyle.

Bruce Boxleitner (b. 1950), Class of 1990. Youthful Bruce Boxleitner is a familiar face to TV and film fans thanks to his body of work, which stretches from the mid-1970s to the present day. Boxleitner is best known for his roles on television in *How the West Was Won* (which starred WOWS honoree James Arness), *Bring 'em Back Alive*, *Scarecrow and Mrs. King*, *Babylon 5*, and in *The Gambler* films with Kenny Rogers. He also starred in the *Tron* series of science-fiction films. For many years, Boxleitner was married to Melissa Gilbert, who is also honored on the Walk of Western Stars. Below is the poster for *How the West Was Won*, with Boxleitner third from right.

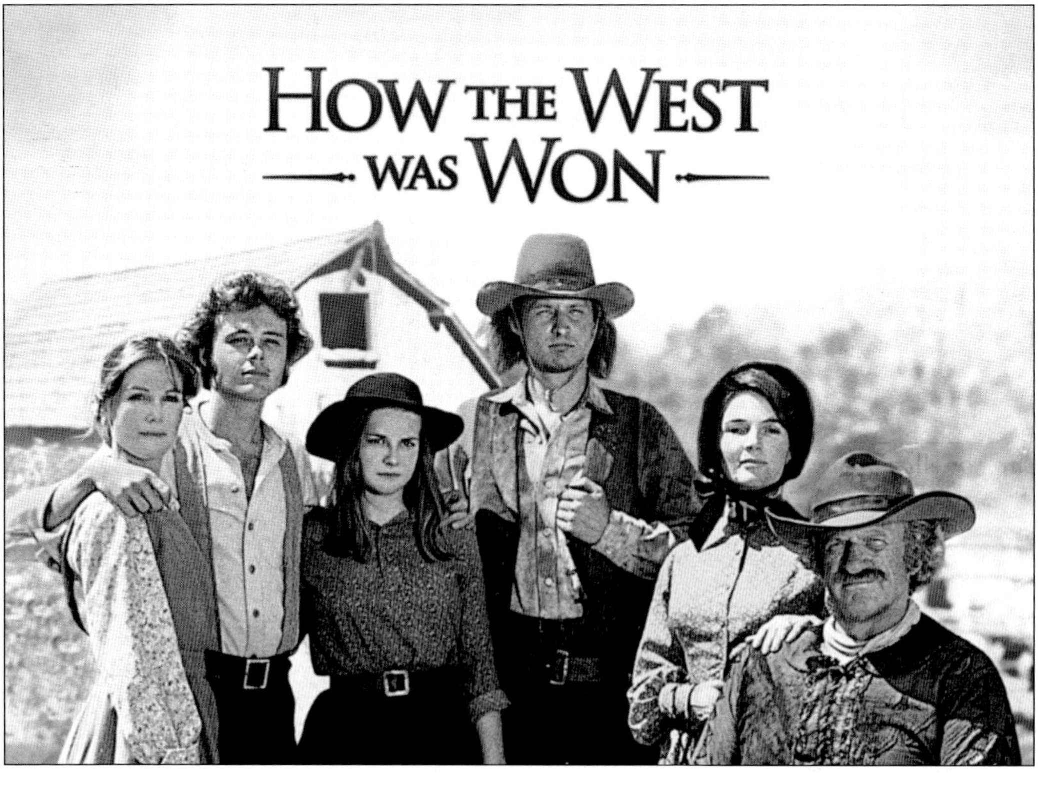

Lee Horsley (b. 1955), Class of 1990. Where better for an avid outdoorsman and Western television star to have been born than Muleshoe, Texas? This was the case for Lee Horsley, who began his acting career on stage before starring in several shows in the 1980s and 1990s like *Nero Wolfe*, *Matt Houston*, *Paradise*, *Bodies of Evidence*, and *Hawkeye*. Horsley was also seen in the cult film *The Sword and the Sorcerer* and narrated the audiobook edition of Larry McMurtry's *Lonesome Dove*. Horsley has been cast by director Quentin Tarantino in two films in recent years: *Django Unchained* and *The Hateful Eight*. At right is a publicity photo from the television series *Paradise* (1988–1991).

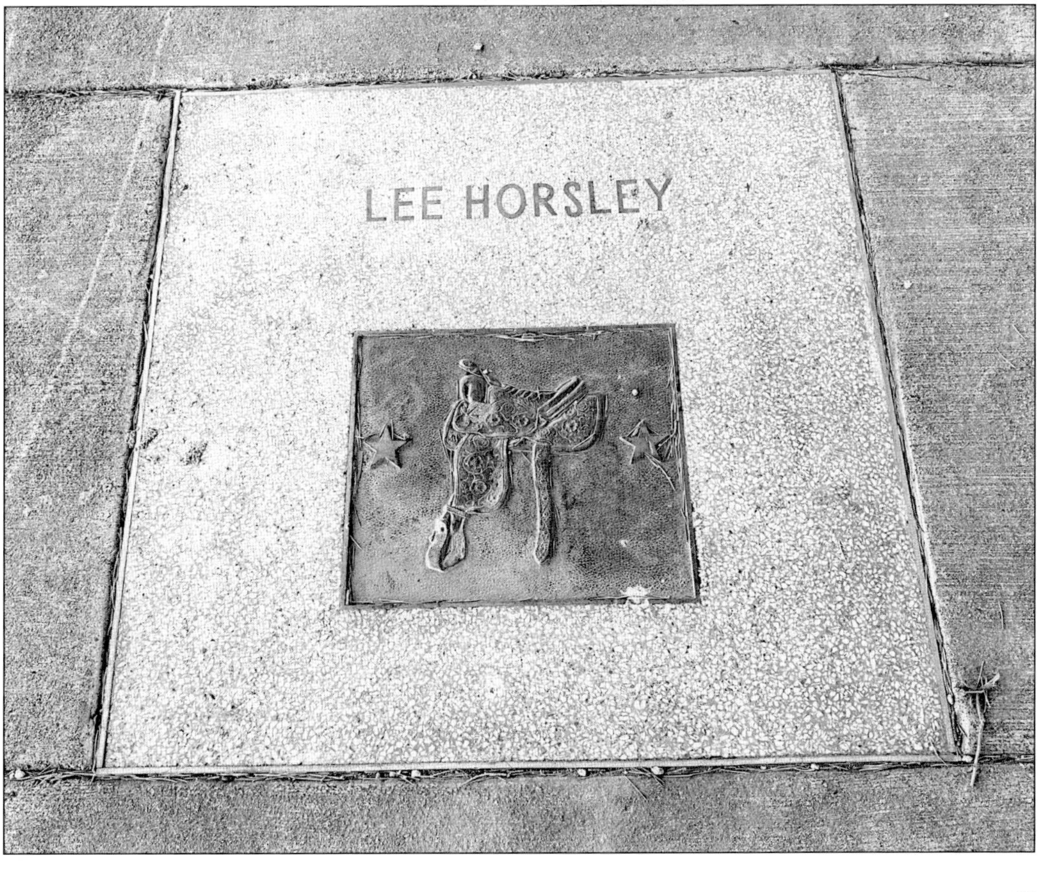

CLIFFIE STONE (1917–1998), CLASS OF 1990. Country music legend Cliffie Stone, born Clifford Snyder, was a singer, musician, disk jockey, record producer, author, and music publisher. As the host of the *Hometown Jamboree* radio program from 1946 to 1960, he helped launch the careers of dozens of country musicians. The multitasking Stone was signed by Capitol Records in Hollywood as both an artist and as head of their country and western division. Toward the end of his life, he kept busy directing local legend Gene Autry's vast publishing empire. Stone was awarded a star on the Hollywood Walk of Fame at the corner of Sunset Boulevard and Vine Street and was inducted into the Country Music Hall of Fame in 1989. He lived in Newhall for many years.

MORGAN WOODWARD (1925–2019), CLASS OF 1990. Morgan Woodward appeared in over 250 episodes during a long career in television. He is perhaps best remembered for his role as Punk Anderson on the long-running prime-time soap *Dallas*. Woodward also starred earlier in his career as Shotgun Gibbs in *The Life and Legend of Wyatt Earp* and made 19 guest appearances on *Gunsmoke*, the most by any actor. Woodward also guest-starred on two episodes of the original *Star Trek* series. On screen, his most iconic performance was as the sadistic Boss Godfrey, who torments Paul Newman in *Cool Hand Luke* (1967), as seen below.

Hoyt Axton (1938–1999), Class of 1991. Folk and country and western singer-songwriter Hoyt Axton came by his talents naturally. His mother, Mae Boren Axton, cowrote the rock 'n' roll classic "Heartbreak Hotel" for Elvis Presley. Axton made the occasional film and television appearance during his career and composed several popular jingles for products like Busch Beer and the Big Mac. But it was as a songwriter that Axton truly left his mark. He wrote hits for performers ranging from Three Dog Night ("Joy to the World" and "Never Been to Spain") to Ringo Starr ("No-No Song"). He also scored hits for the Kingston Trio ("Greenback Dollar") and composed songs covered by artists such as John Denver, Steppenwolf, Waylon Jennings, Glen Campbell, and Anne Murray. Axton died after suffering two heart attacks in 1999. In 2007, both he and his mother were posthumously inducted into the Oklahoma Music Hall of Fame.

George Montgomery (1916–2000), Class of 1991. Multi-talented George Montgomery Letz was raised on a ranch in Montana, where he learned to ride and herd cattle. In 1937, after only two days in Hollywood, he landed a job as a stuntman in a Greta Garbo film. For the next several years, Montgomery, who *Life* magazine once described as "superlatively handsome," had bit parts and performed stunts in several Western films. During the early 1940s, Montgomery played leading man roles opposite some of Hollywood's biggest starlets, like Betty Grable, Carole Landis, Maureen O'Hara, and Ginger Rogers. After serving in World War II, he was demoted to low-budget Western films before finding steady work on television. Montgomery was briefly engaged to Hedy Lamarr and was married for 20 years to Dinah Shore. He not only acted and directed but was a master bronze sculptor and ran his own cabinet-making business. In this image, Montgomery is awarded his saddle in 1991.

Hugh O'Brian (1925–2016), Class of 1991. Born Hugh Charles Krampe in Rochester, New York, Hugh O'Brian was best known for his starring role in the top-ten television series *The Life and Legend of Wyatt Earp.* After serving as the Marine Corps's youngest drill instructor during World War II, O'Brian planned to attend Yale to study law but decided on acting instead. He made dozens of film and television appearances and has the distinction of being the last man ever killed on screen by John Wayne in Wayne's final film, *The Shootist.* After a nine-day visit with Dr. Albert Schweitzer in Africa, O'Brian was inspired to create the Hugh O'Brian Youth Leadership Foundation, a nonprofit youth leadership program for high school scholars. Since its inception, 500,000 students have participated in the foundation. O'Brian is pictured here in 1960 with Princess Soraya, the former wife of the shah of Iran.

Denver Pyle (1920–1997), Class of 1991. Denver Pyle began his long film and television career shortly after World War II, appearing in dozens of productions across multiple genres. A few of his most familiar roles were as Briscoe Darling on *The Andy Griffith Show*, Mad Jack on *The Life and Times of Grizzly Adams*, and most famously as Uncle Jesse, the patriarch of the Duke family on TV's *The Dukes of Hazzard*. A wise investor, Pyle made more money from his oil wells than he did from 30 years of acting. Incidentally, his older brother Willis was a noted animator for Walt Disney and United Productions of America (UPA), where he helped create one of UPA's most famous characters, Mr. Magoo. At right is a publicity photo from *The Dukes of Hazzard*, with Tom Wopat (left), Pyle (seated), and John Schneider. Below is a still from *The Andy Griffith Show*, with Frances Bavier.

Virginia Mayo (1920–2005), Class of 1992. Screen legend Virginia Mayo was one of the biggest stars of Hollywood's Golden Era. Mayo, born Virginia Clara Jones in St. Louis, began her performing career in vaudeville as a singer and dancer. Mayo's talent and stunning good looks soon landed her in Hollywood, where she was cast in starring roles by 1944. Two years later, she earned rave reviews for her performance in *The Best Years of Our Lives*, which won Best Picture. Mayo also shined brightly as Jimmy Cagney's scheming wife in *White Heat*, as well as in several Westerns around this time opposite Joel McCrea, Burt Lancaster, Kirk Douglas, Clint Walker, and Randolph Scott. In addition to her Walk of Western Stars saddle, Mayo also received both a star on the St. Louis Walk of Fame and the Hollywood Walk of Fame, where she was one of the first honorees.

MONTIE MONTANA (1910–1998), CLASS OF 1992. For 60 years, Tournament of Roses Parade viewers watched Montie Montana entertain the crowds by riding his horse and performing rope tricks along Colorado Boulevard in Pasadena. Born in the state of Montana as Owen Harlen Mickel, Montana enjoyed a 40-year career on screen as an actor, stuntman, and trick rider and roper, often in uncredited roles. He appeared briefly in the Western classics *The Man who Shot Liberty Valance* and *Hud*. A popular rodeo performer, Montana was inducted into several rodeo halls of fame, including the ProRodeo Hall of Fame in 1994.

Jane Russell (1921–2011), Class of 1992. Actress, producer, nightclub singer, and sex symbol Jane Russell made her screen debut in 1943 in Howard Hughes's racy Western *The Outlaw*, a role that made her a star. She later played Calamity Jane in *The Paleface* opposite Bob Hope, who in referencing her ample bosom, once introduced her as "the two and only, Jane Russell!" (In the 1970s, Russell became the pitchwoman for Playtex 18-hour bras.) *Gentlemen Prefer Blondes*, her most famous film, co-starred Marilyn Monroe. The following year, she scored a two million–selling single with "Do Lord," which she recorded with members of her Hollywood Christian group who would regularly meet at her home for Bible study. In the 1950s, Russell created a charity called World Adoption International Fund to aid Americans in adopting foreign children, adopting two boys and a girl herself. Her autobiography, *Jane Russell: My Path and My Detours*, was published in 1985. Seen here is a publicity shot from 1943's *The Outlaw*.

Sam Elliott (b. 1944), Class of 1993. Tall and lanky, with a whisk-broom mustache and a deep, canyon-filling voice, Sam Elliott is to many the personification of the perfect Western man. Elliott was born in 1944 in Sacramento and moved with his family to Portland, Oregon, when he was 13. He began in Westerns in the late 1960s, appearing briefly in *Butch Cassidy and the Sundance Kid*, where he met his future wife and WOWS honoree Katherine Ross. The year that he and Ross got their saddles on the Walk of Western Stars, Elliott appeared on screen as Gen. John Buford in *Gettysburg* and as Virgil Earp in *Tombstone*. In 2018, Elliott was nominated for a Best Supporting Actor Oscar for his role in the remake of *A Star Is Born*. In addition, he has been nominated for two Golden Globes during his career, as well as two Primetime Emmys.

Jack Palance (1919–2006), Class of 1993. Tall and talented tough-guy Jack Palance was born Volodymyr Palahniuk in Pennsylvania to Ukrainian immigrants. His father was a coal miner. Palance's chiseled, serpentine face leant itself to roles as on-screen heavies. It was reported early in his career that his unique look came as the result of reconstructive surgery after a plane crash in World War II—a story that Palance later revealed was the creation of studio press agents. Palance was nominated for a Best Supporting Actor Oscar in *Sudden Fear*, only his third film, where he played a coal miner like his father. He was nominated for the same award the following year for playing a hired gun in the classic Western *Shane*. In 1991, Palance finally won the Best Supporting Actor award after his third nomination for his portrayal of Curly Washburn in the comedy *City Slickers*. He famously did a series of one-handed pushups on stage after accepting his Oscar. Novelist Chuck Palahniuk, the author of *Fight Club*, is a distant relative of Palance. This is a publicity photo of Palance from *City Slickers* (1991).

KATHARINE ROSS (B. 1940), CLASS OF 1993. When Katharine Ross comes to mind, many are immediately transported to images of her and Paul Newman riding a bicycle in the dirt in *Butch Cassidy and the Sundance Kid*, with "Raindrops Keep Fallin' on My Head" playing in the background. It was on that film that she met her future husband (and fellow Walk of Western Stars honoree) Sam Elliot, whom she married 15 years later. Readers may also remember her Best Supporting Actress–nominated role in *The Graduate*. Renowned for her beauty, Ross also played the daughter of John Wayne in *Hellfighters* and the daughter-in-law of James Stewart in the Western *Shenandoah*. Ross also starred in *The Singing Nun* and *The Stepford Wives*, and appeared with her husband, Sam Elliot, in the Louis L'Amour–based Western TV movie *Conagher*.

WOODY STRODE (1914–1994), CLASS OF 1993. Black Filmmakers Hall of Famer Woodrow Wilson Woolwine Strode was a world-class decathlete at UCLA, where he also played football, sharing the same backfield with Jackie Robinson, and was drafted by the NFL's Los Angeles Rams in 1946. His screen career began when he was cast as an African warrior in a 1951 jungle film that required him to shave his head—a look he maintained for the remainder of his career. Sheriff Woody from *Toy Story* is said to have been named after him.

Stuart Whitman (1928–2020), Class of 1993. Stuart Whitman's long television and screen career began after his discharge from the US Army Corps of Engineers, where he boxed as a lightweight and won 31 of his 32 bouts. Whitman appeared in bit parts in two science-fiction classics in 1951: *When Worlds Collide* and *The Day the Earth Stood Still*. A familiar face to television and film viewers for the next five decades, Whitman's thriving side hustle as a real estate developer allowed him the luxury of only accepting parts that he wanted. In 1961, Whitman starred in *The Mark*, for which he was nominated for a Best Actor Oscar for his controversial portrayal of a child molester. That same year, he teamed up with John Wayne in *The Comancheros*, one of his many Western roles, and later appeared in several popular features, including the war film *The Longest Day* and the comedy *Those Magnificent Men in their Flying Machines*. Whitman retired from acting in 2000 and died of skin cancer in 2020. Seen here is a publicity photo from *The Comancheros* with Whitman and Ina Balin.

Three

THE 2000S

After a seven-year hiatus, new saddles were again added to the sidewalks of Newhall. The year 2000 brought an end to the honoree drought with a total of three new inductees, as part of 33 for the entire decade. This photograph is of local Santa Clarita Valley legend Harry "Dobe" Carey, who received his WOWS saddle in 2005.

Peter Brown (1935–2016), Class of 2000. Pierre de Lappe was pumping gas at a Hollywood service station when he was discovered by studio head Jack Warner. Later, as Peter Brown, he went to work at Warner's studio, eventually landing the leading role of deputy Johnny McKay in the classic ABC Western series *Lawman*. From there, he portrayed Texas ranger Chad Cooper in the NBC Western action-comedy series *Laredo*. Brown also appeared in TV Westerns such as *Maverick*, *Cheyenne*, *The Virginian*, *Sugarfoot*, and *Colt .45*, as well as in several soap operas. Brown learned acting in Alaska while in the US Army, where he wrote plays to entertain the troops. From there, he honed his skills in an acting program in Los Angeles, where, luckily for him, he also pumped gas. This is a publicity photo from *Summer Magic* (1963) with Hayley Mills.

Don Edwards (b. 1939), Class of 2000. Grammy-nominated balladeer and frequent Cowboy Festival performer Don Edwards taught himself to play the guitar and learned showmanship from his vaudevillian father. He left home at 16 to work in the Texas oil fields and began performing a few years later at the recently opened Six Flags Over Texas theme park. Edwards, who has carved out quite a career retelling lots of tales sung on lots of trails, has had two of his albums included in the Folklore Archives of the Library of Congress.

Richard Farnsworth (1920–2000), Class of 2000. Richard Farnsworth's stunt career began when he discovered he could make more money utilizing his horsemanship on a film set rather than on the polo field where he worked. Farnsworth quickly gained work on such diverse films as Gary Cooper's *The Adventures of Marco Polo*, Cary Grant's *Gunga Din*, and *A Day at the Races*, starring the Marx Brothers. Farnsworth appeared in uncredited acting roles in *Gone with the Wind* and *The Ten Commandments* and only received his first acting credit at the advanced age of 43. He drove a chariot with Kirk Douglas on *Spartacus* and, shortly thereafter, co-founded the Stuntmen's Association. By the 1980s, Farnsworth had appeared in *Roots*, *The Grey Fox*, *The Natural*, and as Matthew Cuthbert in *Anne of Green Gables*. Farnsworth, with his trademark mustache and blue eyes, was nominated twice for Oscars: first in 1978 for Best Supporting Actor for his performance in *Comes a Horseman* and in 1999 for *The Straight Story*, which earned him a Best Actor nomination. (He is also in the running for best mustache on the walk, but he has stiff competition from Wilford Brimley, Waddie Mitchell, and Sam Elliott.) Farnsworth is seen here in a publicity photo from *The Grey Fox* (1982).

Wilford Brimley (1934–2020), Class of 2001. Walrus-mustached Wilford Brimley's face may immediately conjure up images of Quaker Oats. For years, Brimley's homespun looks and kind voice made him the perfect pitchman for the product. What many may not know is that Brimley once featured his singing chops on an album of jazz standards and that he was an accomplished harmonica and poker player who once served as a bodyguard for Howard Hughes. What most people do know is that Brimley was first and foremost an actor whose most famous screen roles were as Pop Fisher in *The Natural* and Ben Luckett in *Cocoon*. Brimley dropped out of high school to join the US Marines and later began his Hollywood career as a stuntman and blacksmith for Westerns. His first screen appearance came in an uncredited role in 1969's *True Grit*. On the small screen, he gained fame as Horace Brimley on television's *The Waltons*. And though it may be hard to imagine, he appears on screen without his trademark mustache in the 1982 horror flick *The Thing*.

Jo Anne Darcy (1931–2017), Class of 2001. The Walk of Western Stars honors a passel of Western actors, actresses, stunt people, musicians, and one politician—Jo Anne Darcy. The concept of what would eventually become the Walk of Western Stars was begun by this forward-thinking Saugus resident in 1975 and was originally known as the Western Celebrities Luncheon/Dinner. The physical walk came in 1981 under the name the Western Walk of Fame, which changed a few years later to its current name. In addition to her work emblazoned on Newhall's sidewalks in bronze and terrazzo tile, Darcy was also instrumental in merging the towns of Saugus, Valencia, Newhall, and Canyon Country together into the city of Santa Clarita. She served as mayor of the new city several times, as well as on the city council and chamber of commerce. In addition to her Walk of Western Stars plaque, her name can be found on the Jo Anne Darcy Canyon Country Library. Darcy is pictured at her saddle's unveiling in 2001, with Santa Clarita City Council member Laurene Weste at right.

Linda Gray (b. 1940), Class of 2001. While she may have lived in Santa Clarita for many years, Linda Gray was famous for being from "Dallas," having starred on the hit television show of the same name. On *Dallas*, she portrayed Sue Ellen, the long-suffering wife of J.R. Ewing, and has enjoyed many roles before and since, including parts on *McCloud*, *Models Inc.*, *Bonanza: The Return*, and *Dallas: J.R. Returns*. Gray starred in the stage version of *The Graduate* in 2001 as Mrs. Robinson, which was a return for her to the famous 1967 screen role, in a way—those are actually Linda Gray's legs on the famous poster. Here, Gray (left) is seen with Jo Anne Darcy at their WOWS induction in 2001.

Herb Jeffries (1913–2014), Class of 2001. Herb Jeffries, the "Bronze Buckaroo," was the first African American singing cowboy. Born Umberto Alexander Valentino in Detroit, Jeffries first made a name for himself as a singer. Louis Armstrong encouraged him to move to Chicago, where he worked with Earl Hines and Duke Ellington. His recording of "Flamingo" sold several million copies. In the 1930s, Jeffries filmed a series of Western-themed "race films" intended for black audiences. Jeffries died in 2014 after turning 100. He is pictured at the TCM Classic Film Festival in Hollywood in 2011.

ALEX CORD (B. 1933), CLASS OF 2002. Alex Cord was born far from the West in New York, where he contracted polio at age 12 and spent time in the hospital in an iron lung. Turning lemons into lemonade, Cord was sent to Wyoming to recuperate, where he learned to rodeo ride, becoming the horseman he always dreamed of being. Disaster struck again when he was thrown from a horse and hospitalized back in New York. This time, he used his convalescence to receive a degree in literature from New York University. This led to acting in Shakespearean plays, and the rest, as they say in Hollywood, is history. With his acting and riding skills, Cord soon earned parts in *Laramie*, *Branded*, *Gunsmoke*, the 1966 remake of *Stagecoach*, *Walker: Texas Ranger*, and a starring role in the 1980s series *Airwolf*. Cord's ability to overcome early misfortune is a testament to his perseverance and how tragedy can sometimes pave the way to success. Cord is pictured on location for a film shoot.

John Schneider (b. 1960), Class of 2002. When it came time to fill the role of Bo Duke for a new show called *The Dukes of Hazzard*, the casting call went out for a 25-year-old southerner. The guy who ended up getting the part was a 17-year-old New Yorker. But it just so happened that John Schneider, the 17-year-old in question, had attended high school in Georgia so he could fake the accent and had no qualms about lying about his age. The show, which lasted seven seasons (and was often filmed in Newhall), made Schneider a star. Schneider went on to enjoy a recurring role as Superman's dad in *Smallville* and over a hundred other screen appearances. Not just a handsome face, Schneider also has a fine singing voice and has recorded several hits on the country charts.

Peggy Stewart (1923–2019), Class of 2002. At the age of seven, Peggy Stewart journeyed from her home in Georgia to California to attend her uncle's wedding and decided to stay and live with her grandmother. At this early age, she wanted to be an actor even though she did not come from a showbiz family. (As she told the authors, "My father was a bookie, if you want to call that an actor!") After hitting the ground running at age 14 playing Joel McCrea's daughter in *Wells Fargo*, Stewart went on to act on screen dozens of times in a career that lasted well into this century. Below, Stewart and Gene Autry are seen in a still from *Trail to San Antone* (1947).

PEGGY STEWART. Peggy Stewart appeared in 32 films for Republic Studios, often in strong roles that displayed her equestrian skills. Along the way, she appeared alongside luminaries like Bette Davis, Jackie Cooper, and fellow WOWS honorees Gene Autry and Dale Evans. More recently, Stewart was seen on television in episodes of *The Office* and *Seinfeld*. This gracious, hilarious lady passed away in 2019 at the age of 95. She is greatly missed by all who were lucky enough to have known her. Above, Stewart is being interviewed by the authors on *SCV In The Movies* in 2013. Below, Stewart is seen in a publicity photo from *Marshal of Laredo* (1945) with Wild Bill Elliott.

WILLIAM BOYD (1895–1972), CLASS OF 2003. William Boyd became a lunchbox legend by playing the character Hopalong Cassidy in more than 60 features, which is a record for any actor portraying a single role. The character Hopalong Cassidy began in a series of short stories by author Clarence E. Mulford and was originally a rugged, rough-and-tumble type, who hopped along on his wooden leg. When William Boyd took over the role, he transformed the character into a do-gooder who kids grew up hoping to emulate. Boyd notably went against the Hollywood Western grain by wearing all black. At left, Boyd poses with one of his fans in 1950. Below, Boyd appears as Hopalong Cassidy in a publicity photo from one of his many Westerns.

William Boyd. After starring in dozens of Hopalong Cassidy sagas, William Boyd mortgaged everything to purchase the rights to the "Hoppy" films and character. Barely able to survive financially, he and his wife, Grace, lived for a time at Gene Autry's Melody Ranch in Newhall. When television came along, Boyd's big gamble paid off in a major way when he used the medium to develop new shows featuring his character, earning him millions. In the early 1950s, Boyd backed an amusement park in the Venice area of Los Angeles, which was known as Hoppyland, pictured below.

Bruce Dern (b. 1936), Class of 2003. Younger folks may recognize Bruce Dern from his appearances in the Quentin Tarantino films *Once upon a Time in Hollywood*, *The Hateful Eight*, and *Django Unchained*, while old-timey Western fans may know him from *Hang 'em High*, *Support Your Local Sheriff*, *They Shoot Horses, Don't They?*, and *Pat Garrett and Billy the Kid*. Dern, who often played unhinged movie bad guys, appeared in two of Alfred Hitchcock's final films, *Marnie* and *Family Plot*, and racked up a couple of firsts during his career. In the film *The Cowboys*, he became the first villain to ever kill a character played by John Wayne. In 2010, when he, his ex-wife actress Diane Ladd, and their daughter actress Laura Dern received Hollywood Walk of Fame stars, it was the first time that an entire acting family had been honored in the same ceremony. Dern is seen here in a still from *Once upon a Time in Hollywood* (2019).

Riders in the Sky (formed 1977), Class of 2003. What do you get when you mix beautiful Western harmonies sung by talented musicians, toss in some Texas-worthy Western garb, and add lots of laughs from a group of guys who introduce themselves as "Ranger Doug, the Idol of American Youth," "Woody Paul, the King of the Cowboy Fiddlers," "Too Slim, the Man of a Thousand Hats," and "Joey, the Cowpolka King"? The one and only correct answer is Riders in the Sky. The Riders keep alive the classic Western sounds of performers like Gene Autry, Roy Rogers, and *Sons of the Pioneers* in an engaging, hilarious way. Riders in the Sky formed in 1977 and have made more than 8,000 appearances, produced more than 40 albums, and had their own television show on CBS for two seasons. They also provided music for the Disney-Pixar film *Toy Story 2*.

Buck Taylor (b. 1938), Class of 2003. Some may remember him as gunsmith Newly O'Brien in *Gunsmoke* or, if of the younger persuasion, as Wes Claiborne in the movie *Cowboys & Aliens* or as Emmett Walsh in the TV series *Yellowstone*. There are over a hundred other roles played by Buck Taylor that one may be familiar with. Taylor is also an artist who captures beautiful images of the West in watercolors. The son of actor Dub Taylor, Buck was born in Hollywood and grew up around "the industry," but was studying to be an artist at USC when the opportunity to appear in *Gunsmoke* came calling. He appeared in over a hundred episodes, and his character progressed from gunsmith to deputy. These days, Taylor splits his time between acting and art, promoting the West, and honoring our military and peace officers. Seen here is Taylor (left) in a still from the film *Wild Wild West* (1999).

Keith Carradine (b. 1949), Class of 2004. Part of the Carradine family acting dynasty, Keith Carradine began his career on the stage, once starring with his father John in a production of *Tobacco Road.* He also appeared alongside his brothers Robert and David in the film *The Long Riders.* Carradine has often been seen portraying famous Western figures such as Buffalo Bill Cody in *Wild Bill*, and Wild Bill Hickock in the HBO series *Deadwood.* He has also been seen regularly on television in *Fargo* and *Madam Secretary*, where he played the president of the United States. Known for his laid-back yet intense style on screen, off screen, Carradine is known as a nice, approachable guy. Carradine, like his brother David, is a musician. He won both Academy and Golden Globe awards for Best Song for his 1975 hit "I'm Easy" from the film *Nashville.* Here, Keith Carradine (left) and author Bill West are at the 2004 WOWS induction ceremony.

Melissa Gilbert (b. 1964), Class of 2004. Beloved for her portrayal of Laura Ingalls on *Little House on the Prairie*, Melissa Gilbert said that portraying Ingalls *was* her childhood and that being on the set was like being in summer camp. Gilbert played the role for nearly a decade on television from 1974–1983, and in 2009, she played Caroline "Ma" Ingalls in the musical stage version of *Little House*. In 2014, she penned a cookbook dedicated to fans called *My Prairie Cookbook: Memories and Frontier Food from My Little House to Yours*. Additionally, Gilbert starred in TV movies like *The Diary of Anne Frank* and *The Miracle Worker*, performed voice work as Batgirl in *Batman: The Animated Series*, and appeared on *Dancing with the Stars*. In addition to acting roles, Gilbert was the two-term president of the Screen Actors Guild and ran for US Congress in 2016, winning in the primary before bowing out of the race for health reasons. Gilbert (far left) is seen in a publicity photo of the cast of *Little House on the Prairie*.

Loren Janes (1931–2017), Class of 2004. Handsome, daring, and innovative stuntman Loren Janes doubled for Jack Nicholson, Paul Newman, Frank Sinatra, Charles Bronson, and John Wayne during his long, storied career. He was Steve McQueen's double for over two decades, including many of the famous car chase scenes in *Bullitt*. He even doubled for female stars like Esther Williams and Debbie Reynolds. Janes's many screen appearances included *The Ten Commandments*, *Spartacus*, *The Magnificent Seven*, *How the West Was Won*, and *McClintock*! He was an Olympic athlete and a co-founder of the Stuntmen's Association of Motion Pictures & Television. Due to his skill and calculated approach to his craft, he will forever be remembered as one of the principal engineers of modern stunt work. Sadly, less than a year before his death, Janes's home was lost in the deadly Sand Fire that tore through the Santa Clarita Valley in 2016. Not only did he lose his residence, but most of the treasured memorabilia he had collected over his film career. Janes (left) and Steve McQueen are pictured on the set of *The Hunter* (1980).

Buck Page (1922–2006), Class of 2004. In 1936, a 13-year-old guitarist named Buck Page spied the Zane Grey novel *Riders of the Purple Sage* on his brother's shelf and immediately had a name for his new musical group. It turned out that there was another band in California with the same name at the time, but since Page was on the East Coast, it is doubtful he ever knew of its existence. Page's brother joined him in the new band, and soon they were a hit, playing Western music on the radio. While Page was in the Navy during World War II, another version of the Riders with singer Foy Willing began performing in California. Willing's band disbanded in 1952, and Page revived his Riders in the early 1960s, performing with the band until shortly before his death. The Riders still perform today using former members of both Page's and Willing's versions of the groups. The confusion caused by the various incarnations of the band gets even worse when you add the existence of the classic country-rock band New Riders of the Purple Sage.

Powers Boothe (1948–2017), Class of 2005. An unforgettable presence on screen, Powers Boothe first gained fame in the 1980 television movie *The Guyana Tragedy* in a riveting Emmy Award–winning performance as cult leader Jim Jones. He followed up this performance by playing many other unforgettable characters like Lamar Wyatt in the TV Series *Nashville*, Alexander Haig in *Nixon*, Curly Bill Brocious in *Tombstone*, and saloon owner Cy Tolliver in HBO's *Deadwood*, which was filmed at Newhall's Melody Ranch. Boothe played the starring role in the TV series *Philip Marlow, Private Eye*, and had recurring roles in *24* and *Agents of S.H.I.E.L.D.* He was married to his college sweetheart, Pam Cole, from 1969 until his death in 2017. Boothe was laid to rest in the town of Deadwood, but in the state of Texas, not the one in South Dakota that he helped make famous. Boothe is seen here in a still from *Deadwood*.

Harry Carey Jr. (1921–2012), Class of 2005. Born and schooled in Saugus, Harry Carey Jr., known to his friends as "Dobe" (pronounced "Dobey," for the red adobe color of his hair), was a respected character actor who appeared in over 90 films. Carey was the son of Harry Carey Sr. and Olive Carey, two great Western actors from the silent and early sound eras. Despite his lineage, Carey did not start out as an actor but as a medical corpsman in the Navy. It was during his service that he met director John Ford, who hired him to play in several Western classics, including *The Searchers*, where he appeared with his real-life mother, Olive Carey, who played his mother in the film. Carey often worked alongside John Wayne and appeared in the 1993 Western hit *Tombstone*. He was married to Marilyn Fix, the daughter of Western actor Paul Fix, for 68 years until his death. At the Carey family ranch in Saugus, which today is the Rancho Tesoro Adobe park, visitors can still see the name "Dobe" carved into a surrounding wall. Carey is pictured in this 1940 publicity photo from *She Wore a Yellow Ribbon*.

Graham Greene (b. 1952), Class of 2005. With over a hundred screen credits since 1976, Native American Graham Green is a prolific, skilled, reliable actor. Born at the Six (Iroquois) Nations Reserve in Canada—the same birthplace as *The Lone Ranger's* Tonto, Jay Silverheels—Greene's background made him the perfect, authentic choice for many Native American roles in movies such as *The Green Mile* and *Dances with Wolves*, for which he was nominated for an Oscar for Best Supporting Actor, and in television shows like *Northern Exposure*. Greene has also been seen on screen in many non–Native American roles. According to the Internet Movie Database, when asked if he felt he had been typecast, he replied, "I've played all kinds of things. I played an old Jewish man in a furniture store in theater. I played the ghost of a black transvestite. I've played British soldiers. I've played French soldiers. I've played New York cops. I've played lawyers. So, no." Above, Greene is seen in a scene from *Dances with Wolves* (1990).

Jack Williams (1921–2007), Class of 2005. Jack Williams was a stuntman who specialized in both riding horses and falling with horses. When directors needed to show a horse and rider falling together, Williams was the man they called. He had learned this rare skill from his father, who was a real Montana cowboy, and from his mother, a famous rodeo trick rider. Williams's first film appearance came at age four, when he was tossed between riders from horse to horse in a 1926 silent film. A handsome, muscular man, Williams was often called upon to double for famous actors, including Errol Flynn, Kirk Douglas, and Charlton Heston. He made more than 80 screen appearances, the last coming in 1999's *Wild Wild West*, which was partially shot in Santa Clarita's Placerita Canyon. Like fellow Walk of Western Stars honoree Harry Dean Stanton, Williams fought at the Battle of Okinawa in World War II. He appeared in several stellar Westerns, along with a few less-than-classics, like 1966's *Billy the Kid vs. Dracula*. John Carradine, the film's star, considered it to be the worst movie he ever acted in.

James Arness (1923–2011), Class of 2006. For 20 years, millions of television viewers invited James Arness into their homes each week. The long-running Western *Gunsmoke*, which filmed for a time in Newhall, made a star of the Minnesota-born actor. Arness made it to Hollywood after being machine-gunned by the Nazis in World War II. After a stint as a beach bum, he landed parts as a "heavy" due to his imposing six-foot-seven frame. At right, Dennis Weaver and Arness (right) are pictured in a still from *Gunsmoke* shot at Melody Ranch. Below is a publicity photo from *Gunsmoke* with, from left to right, Arness, Dennis Weaver, and William "Hopalong Cassidy" Boyd.

James Arness. John Wayne put James Arness under contract and recommended him for the role of Marshal Dillon on *Gunsmoke*. No stranger to Newhall, Arness would film the first six seasons of *Gunsmoke* at Melody Ranch before a brush fire in 1962 burned the ranch to the ground. Arness was initially reluctant to take the part, but Wayne proved persuasive and even filmed a teaser for the first episode to introduce America to the man who would become a generation's friend and role model. Arness is seen here in publicity photos from *Gunsmoke*.

Rhonda Fleming (b. 1923), Class of 2006. What do the Hitchcock suspense film *Suspicion*, the classic film noir *Out of the Past*, the comedy-fantasy *A Connecticut Yankee in King Arthur's Court*, and many Westerns including *Alias Jesse James*, *Gunfight at the O.K. Corral*, and *Pony Express* have in common? They all feature Rhonda Fleming, who was called the "Queen of Technicolor" due to the stunning way she photographed. In the 1955 Western *Tennessee's Partner*, filmed at Chatsworth's Iverson Movie Ranch, she hid behind a recognizable rock formation, which later became known as Rhonda Fleming Rock.

Robert Horton (1924–2016), Class of 2006. Famous for his masculine good looks, Los Angeles native Robert Horton played the lead in the Western television shows *Wagon Train* and *The Man Called Shenandoah*. Horton was also a singer who performed on popular recordings and sang at a command performance for Queen Elizabeth II. Horton starred in nearly 200 episodes of *Wagon Train* but left the show so he could focus more on musical theater. The lead role went to his friend and fellow Walk of Western Stars honoree Robert Fuller, who coincidentally shared the same birthday. Horton (left) and Ward Bond are pictured in a 1958 episode of *Wagon Train*.

Andrew Prine (b. 1936), Class of 2006. Florida-born journeyman actor Andrew Prine supported many of the Hollywood greats, including John Wayne, Dean Martin, James Stewart, Charlton Heston, Deborah Kerr, Raquel Welch, William Holden, Glenn Ford, and Ben Johnson. His film credits include appearances in *The Miracle Worker*, *Bandolero!*, *Chisum*, and *Rooster Cogburn*. On television, he appeared in *Peter Gunn*; *Have Gun–Will Travel*; *Gunsmoke*; *Combat!*; *Ben Casey*; *Dr. Kildare*; *The Virginian*; *Dr. Quinn, Medicine Woman*; and *Walker: Texas Ranger*. Seen here is a publicity photo of Prine (left) and Earl Holliman from *The Wide Country* (1962).

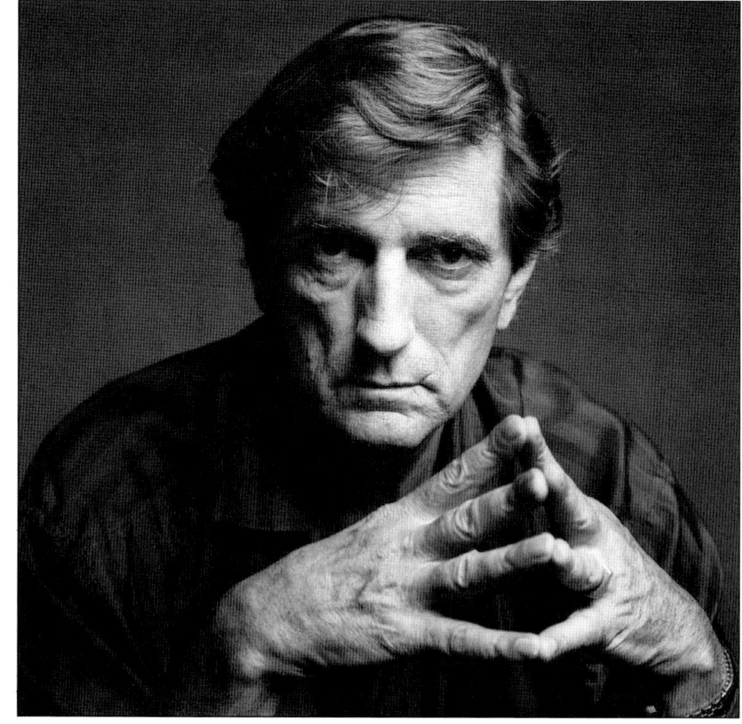

Harry Dean Stanton (1926–2017), Class of 2007. During World War II, Harry Dean Stanton served in the US Navy at the Battle of Okinawa. He later learned the acting trade at the Pasadena Playhouse. Stanton made his screen debut in the 1957 Western *Tomahawk Trail* and went on to play in many Westerns throughout his career, including an appearance in *How the West Was Won*. Stanton can also be seen in *Cool Hand Luke*, *The Godfather: Part II*, *Alien*, and *The Green Mile*, as well as in the cult films *Escape From New York* and *Repo Man*.

Phil Rawlins (1930–2009), Class of 2007. Having lived in the Placerita Canyon area since 1969, stuntman, director, and production manager Phil Rawlins is a true Santa Clarita original. During his film career, Rawlins doubled for Clint Eastwood, Randolph Scott, and Robert Ryan. He also directed television shows such as *F-Troop*, *Cheyenne*, *Bronco*, and *77 Sunset Strip* and was the production manager on *Coma*, *Star Trek: The Motion Picture*, and the first two *Gremlins* films. Rawlins passed away at the age of 79 in Newhall. This is a poster from *Star Trek: The Motion Picture* (1979), one of Rawlins's production manager roles.

Sons of the San Joaquin (formed 1987), Class of 2007. Before the Sons of the San Joaquin discovered they could write, play, and sing beautiful Western music together, they had worked on cattle ranches in California, had successful minor league baseball careers, and been high school teachers in Fresno. The Sons consist of brothers Joe and Jack Hannah and Joe's son Lon. They made their first appearance at the Santa Clarita Cowboy Festival in 1994, and one of their final performances took place at the same festival in 2017.

David Carradine (1936–2009), Class of 2008. Famous for his iconic portrayals of Kwai Chang Caine in TV's *Kung Fu* and Bill in the *Kill Bill* movies, David Carradine also appeared in several Westerns, including starring roles in the television series *Shane*, the TV movie *Mr. Horn*, and alongside his brothers Keith and Robert in the movie *The Long Riders*. Carradine also portrayed Woodie Guthrie in the biopic *Bound for Glory*. Film buffs know that his father was screen legend John Carradine, who appeared in hundreds of films. They may not know that David was also born "John Carradine" but changed his name to avoid confusion with his famous father. In college, Carradine studied music, not acting, and later sang and composed songs for some of his films. Seen here is Carradine as Caine in *Kung Fu*.

Jack Lilley (b. 1933), Class of 2008. A Santa Clarita resident since 1953, stuntman and horse wrangler Jack Lilley appeared in more than 250 movies, including *The Man who Shot Liberty Valance*, *The Shootist*, *Blazing Saddles!*, *Young Guns*, and *Three Amigos*. On television, Lilley appeared in episodes of *Rawhide*, *Gunsmoke*, *Bonanza*, and *High Chaparral*. Lilley was a relative of George Spahn, whose film ranch was the home of the murderous Manson Family. Lilley briefly met Charles Manson and Squeaky Fromme shortly before the infamous Tate/LaBianca murders. Lilley is pictured with his wife, Irene, in 2019 on her 90th birthday at their ranch in Canyon Country.

John Saxon (1936–2020), Class of 2008. John Saxon appeared in nearly 200 roles on TV and film. In Westerns, he played Johnny Portugal in the 1960 film *The Unforgiven*, Chuy Medena in *The Appaloosa*, Dakin McAdam in the TV movie version of *Winchester '73*, and Luis Chama in *Joe Kidd*. Of Italian descent, Saxon's dark complexion often won him roles as Latinos and Native Americans. Saxon spoke fluent Italian and held a black belt in karate, which helped him land a role in Bruce Lee's *Enter the Dragon*. At the Walk of Western Stars event, Saxon told a story about a mishap on the set of *Winchester '73*, where actor Paul Fix was nearly killed by a rifle.

JOEL MCCREA (1905–1990), CLASS OF 2009. With a career spanning over 50 years, Joel McCrea starred in nearly 100 films, half of them Westerns. He shot many of them in the Santa Clarita area at the Andy Jauregui Ranch in Placerita Canyon and at what is now Melody Ranch in Newhall. McCrea's first brush with Hollywood fame came when he delivered a newspaper to the home of silent film cowboy William S. Hart. Hart, who was there with his bulldog Mac, told young Joel, "You must be a pretty good kind of a boy. You're the first one that bulldog hasn't bit." His initial meeting with Bill Hart later came full circle when McCrea was performing in a radio show with Bing Crosby and mentioned on the air how Hart was one of his greatest influences as an actor. Hart happened to be listening and wrote Joel a longhand letter inviting him to come to his ranch in Newhall for a visit. McCrea took him up on the offer, and the two screen cowboys became lifelong friends. McCrea (far right) is pictured in a still from *Wichita* (1955), which was filmed at Melody Ranch.

Four

The 2010s and 2020s

During the decade of the 2010s, a good mixture of Hollywood legends and local Western heroes were enshrined on the Walk of Western Stars. In that time, Western screen icons Gary Cooper, James Stewart, John Ford, Lee Marvin, Charles Bronson, and Steve McQueen were honored along with legendary Santa Clarita Valley locals like Joel Cox, Stuart Hamblen, Diamond Farnsworth, and Renaud and Andre Veluzat. Johnny Crawford was awarded this saddle in 2016.

LLOYD BRIDGES (1913–1998), CLASS OF 2010. One may remember blonde, gravely-voiced Lloyd Bridges from the classic Western *High Noon* (partially filmed at Melody Ranch in Newhall), the iconic television series *Sea Hunt*, or from his role in *Airplane!* that successfully lampooned many of his prior roles. ("Looks like I picked the wrong week to quit [...]"!) Or one might remember him from over 200 other roles in a career that spanned from the 1930s to the 1990s. Above, Bridges is seen in a publicity photo from *Sea Hunt*. At left is Bridges in a publicity photo from the television series *The Loner* (1965–1966).

Lloyd Bridges. Lloyd Bridges was reportedly offered the role of Captain Kirk in the original *Star Trek* series, which later went to William Shatner. Bridges is the patriarch of a famous Hollywood acting family, which includes actors Beau and Jeff Bridges. He and his wife, Dorothy, were married for 59 years until his death in 1998, and on Valentine's Day on each of those years, she would write him a love poem. Above is Bridges in a publicity photo from *Airplane!* (1980). Pictured below are Bridges (center) with his sons Jeff (left) and Beau at an Academy Awards presentation.

GARY COOPER (1901–1961), CLASS OF 2010. One of the Hollywood Golden Era's most legendary leading men, Gary Cooper, with his deliberate delivery, laconic bearing, and masculine "Regular Joe" good looks, is famous for his roles in films like *Mr. Deeds Goes to Town*, *The Westerner*, *Sergeant York*, *Meet John Doe*, *High Noon*, and *The Pride of the Yankees*. Of his over 100 films, about 20 were Westerns, and many of them were shot in the Santa Clarita Valley. Below is a still from 1952's *High Noon*.

GARY COOPER. In 1989, Gary Cooper's image from *High Noon* was used by the Solidarity movement, along with the phrase, "There's a new sheriff in town," as part of Poland's successful fight for independence from the Soviet Union. Like his character Lou Gehrig in *The Pride of the Yankees*, when diagnosed with terminal cancer in 1961, Cooper handled the news with poise and was quoted as saying, "If it is God's will, that's all right, too." Above is Cooper in a still from *High Noon*. Seen below are Cooper (left) and Babe Ruth in a publicity photo from *The Pride of the Yankees* (1942).

Audie Murphy (1925–1971), Class of 2010. The most decorated combat soldier in American history, Audie Murphy enjoyed subsequent fame as a film actor, playing himself in the 1955 film *To Hell and Back*. In that movie, he recreated many of the events of World War II that earned him the Medal of Honor and the Legion of Merit for Valor. What the film did not show is that many of his acts of bravery were performed while Murphy was suffering from the effects of gangrene. Despite his history as a soldier, most of his movie roles were in Westerns, where he benefited from his natural Texas drawl. Below is the poster for the film *To Hell and Back*.

Audie Murphy. Audie Murphy likely suffered from post-traumatic stress disorder in later life. However, despite bankruptcy, he refused to appear in ads for cigarettes or alcohol, not wanting his image to be used in a way that would be harmful to children. Murphy died young at the age of 45 in a plane crash. His gravesite at Arlington National Cemetery (below) is said to be the second most visited after John F. Kennedy's final resting place. To the right is Murphy in a still from *The Red Badge of Courage* (1951). (Below, courtesy of Arlington National Cemetery.)

James Stewart (1908–1997), Class of 2010. The Tom Hanks of his day, Jimmy Stewart was famous for his "everyman" roles in *Mr. Smith Goes to Washington* and *It's a Wonderful Life* and roles in biopics like *The Glenn Miller Story* and *The Spirit of St. Louis*. Stewart also starred in the classic Alfred Hitchcock thrillers *Rear Window* and *Vertigo* and in several brilliant Westerns such as *Destry Rides Again*, *Winchester '73*, *How the West Was Won*, and *The Man who Shot Liberty Valance*. At left, Stewart is pictured with Donna Reed in a still from *It's a Wonderful Life* (1947).

JAMES STEWART. Folks familiar with Jimmy Stewart's film roles may be less aware of his military career. Stewart was drafted into the US Army as a private in 1940. Having previously learned to fly, he rose to the rank of colonel during World War II, flying several combat missions. After the war, Stewart joined the US Air Force Reserves, where he retired as a brigadier general in 1959. Very few actors have reached that rank or higher, although Ronald Reagan was of course commander in chief. Stewart, who was politically conservative, was best friends with liberal Henry Fonda. They maintained their friendship by never talking politics.

JOHN FORD (1894–1973), CLASS OF 2011. Legendary director John Ford filmed four times at the man-made slit in the mountains in Newhall called Beale's Cut. Ford first arrived in 1917 to make *Straight Shooting* and was back for *Three Jumps Ahead* in 1923. He returned the following year for *The Iron Horse* and again in 1939 for *Stagecoach*, the movie that made John Wayne a star. Below is a lobby card from Ford's 1956 classic *The Searchers*.

John Ford. In a 1995 interview, Gene Autry recalled an exchange between John Ford and John Wayne that had taken place decades earlier at Autry's Melody Ranch in Newhall. After Wayne arrived on set late and hungover, Ford publicly berated him, denying him water on the hot set. Secretly, on Ford's orders, Autry slipped Wayne a shot of bourbon. Years later, Wayne sent Autry a signed picture that read, "To Gene Autry. A lot of water has gone under the bridge. And whiskey too." At right, Ford directs a scene for *The Searchers*. Below is a lobby card from *Stagecoach*.

Joel Cox (b. 1942), Class of 2012. By the age of 12, Joel Cox already had a six-year acting career under his belt, despite not particularly enjoying that line of work. His real passion was in the technical side of filmmaking. Cox got a start on his behind-the-camera career after landing a job in the Warner Bros. studio mailroom. Working his way up to film editor, Cox edited his first film with studio boss Jack Warner literally looking over his shoulder. He went on to edit such Hollywood classics as *The Wild Bunch*, but his career reached an even higher level after he worked with Clint Eastwood on *The Outlaw Josey Wales*. This began Cox's 40-plus-year partnership as Eastwood's primary editor that continues to this day. In 1992, Cox took home the Academy Award for Best Editing for Eastwood's Western classic *Unforgiven*. Cox has lived in the Santa Clarita Valley since 1984. From left to right are Bruce Ricker, Clint Eastwood, and Cox at the 2009 Paso Robles Film Festival.

Glenn Ford (1916–2006), Class of 2012. A portion of Glenn Ford's first movie was filmed in Santa Clarita, not far from his plaque on the Walk of Western Stars. The year was 1939, the greatest year of film, and the movie was called *Heaven with a Barbed Wire Fence.* From that beginning in Santa Clarita, Ford went on to appear in many great Westerns, film noirs, and dramas such as *3:10 to Yuma*, *The Rounders*, *Jubal*, *Blackboard Jungle*, and *Gilda*. The Walk of Western Stars was honored to mark the achievements of this great actor in the same town where his more than 50-year/100-film career began. Above, Ford is with Rita Hayworth in a publicity photo from *Gilda* (1946). Below, Ford (right) is seen in a publicity photo from *Heaven with a Barbed Wire Fence* with Richard Conte (left) and Jean Rogers.

Rodolfo Acosta (1920–1974), Class of 2013. Rodolfo Acosta was a Mexican-American character actor. Prior to that, he served in US Naval Intelligence in World War II and met and married his wife in Casablanca during the North African campaign. Acosta always harbored an interest in acting and by his late 20s was landing roles in both Mexican and American films. His rough, chiseled features earned him regular work as outlaws and Native Americans in Western films and on television. Acosta played Silva, the Apache warrior who tries to kill John Wayne in *Hondo*, and Vaquero on *The High Chaparral*. He also appeared in *How the West Was Won*, *The Greatest Story Ever Told*, *The Sons of Katie Elder*, and *Return of the Magnificent Seven*. Acosta worked in Santa Clarita on the film *Apache Warrior* in 1957 and on the television series *Zorro* and *Have Gun–Will Travel*. Rodolfo, who died in 1974, had five children, one of whom is Dante Acosta, who recently served in the California State Assembly and as a Santa Clarita City Council member. Acosta is seen here in a publicity photo from *The Littlest Outlaw* (1955).

STUART HAMBLEN (1908–1989), CLASS OF 2013. Stuart Hamblen was a singer, songwriter, actor, radio star, US presidential candidate, and the first person to ever transport a horse by plane. Born and raised in Texas, Hamblen was the son of the founder of the Evangelical Methodist Church. He and his family would eventually settle in Santa Clarita. Although—or perhaps because—he was raised a preacher's kid, Hamblen was always getting into trouble. Once during a World War II blackout in Los Angeles, the streetlights down Hollywood Boulevard and Vine Street failed to go off, so Hamblen drove down each street in his convertible Cadillac shooting out each light with his rifle. Hamblen developed into a master storyteller and songwriter, penning such classics as "This Ole House," "Remember Me," and "It Is No Secret." Radio's first singing cowboy, Hamblen was awarded a star on the Hollywood Walk of Fame for his popular radio shows. His electric personality and horsemanship secured him roles in Westerns with such greats as Roy Rogers, Gene Autry, Don "Red" Barry (husband of Walk of Western Stars recipient Peggy Stewart), and John Wayne. Seen here is a still from *King of the Forest Rangers* (1946), with Hamblen in the middle.

STUART HAMBLEN. After a wild youth, Stuart Hamblen returned to religion in 1949 with the help of his dear friend Billy Graham. In 1952, Hamblen was the Prohibition Party's candidate for president and took an early lead as the Bible Belt votes were first counted, before eventually losing to Dwight Eisenhower. Since his passing in 1989, Stuart's descendants have kept his memory alive through his music and community service. His daughter Lisa Jaserie served on the Friends of Hart Park board, his grandson Bill Lindsay is the president and CEO of Hamblen Music Company, granddaughter Kim Jaserie is a graphic artist and the vice president of marketing at Hamblen Music, and his great-granddaughter Sarah Lindsay Montalvo is an accomplished singer. Below, Hamblen (second from right) is pictured with a group of friends, including Billy Graham (center).

LEE MARVIN (1924–1987), CLASS OF 2013. Named after his distant relative Confederate general Robert E. Lee, Lee Marvin seemed tailor-made to play the heavy, with his ominous deep baritone voice and scowling demeanor. He employed these talents brilliantly in *The Dirty Dozen*, *Paint Your Wagon*, and *The Man who Shot Liberty Valance*, among numerous other roles. In 1965, the hardboiled New Yorker won a Best Actor Oscar for the film *Cat Ballou*, in which he played two roles. Below is Marvin (pointing) with Clint Eastwood in *Paint Your Wagon* (1969).

Lee Marvin. As a child, Lee Marvin was considered incorrigible and was booted out of several schools. He eventually joined the US Marine Corps at the beginning of World War II and was wounded at the Battle of Saipan near the end of the war. After being discharged, he supported himself with menial jobs, including plumber's apprentice. One day after fixing a toilet at a community theater, he was asked to stand in for an ailing actor. Immediately bitten by the acting bug, he went on to appear in plays in New York, and ultimately made his way to Hollywood. At left is Marvin in boxing gloves. Below is the poster for *The Dirty Dozen* (1967).

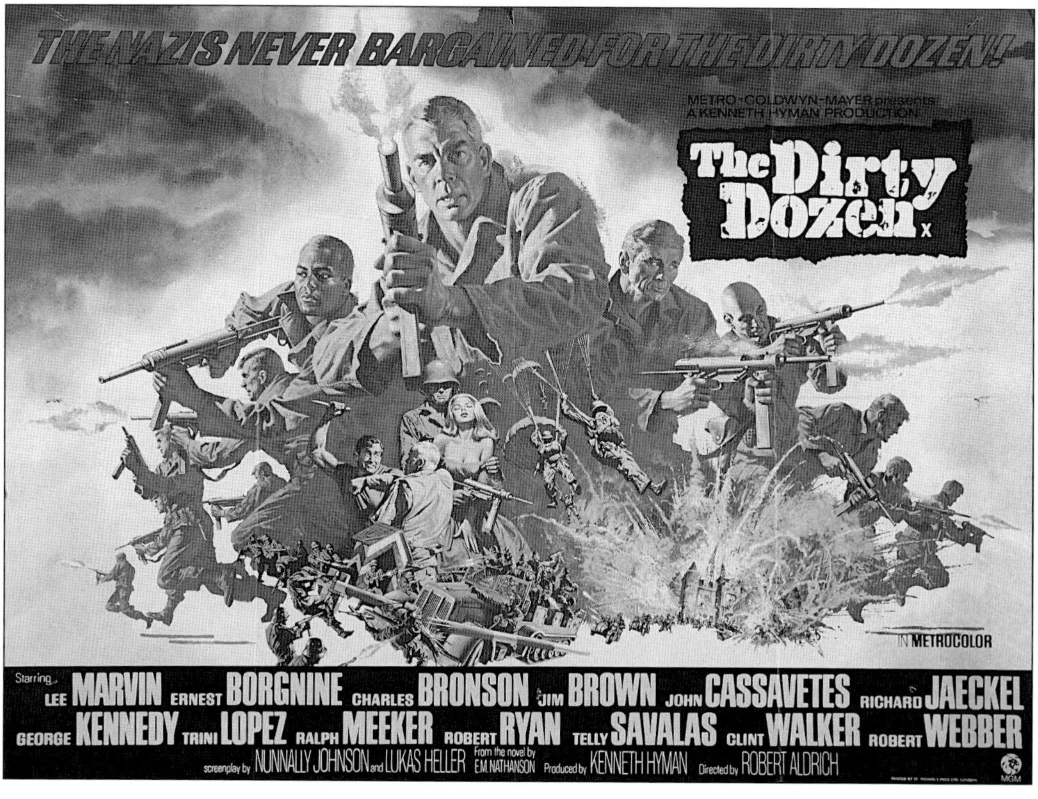

Charles Bronson (1921–2003), Class of 2014. Charles Dennis Buchinsky was born into a poor family of Pennsylvania coal miners with 14 siblings. He would later adopt his stage name from Paramount Studio's Bronson gate and, thereafter, become famous as the legendary Charles Bronson. Muscular and often taciturn and brooding, Bronson usually played quiet bad guys or sometimes good guys with complex motivations. Bronson played the lead in *Machine Gun Kelly*, famously channeled his mining past in *The Great Escape*, and starred as one of *The Dirty Dozen*. He also played an assassin in *The Mechanic* and a vengeful father in the *Death Wish* series of films. Pictured below is Bronson's plaque just outside the KHTS studio on Main Street.

Charles Bronson. Western fans may remember Charles Bronson from *4 for Texas*, *Once upon a Time in the West*, *Chato's Land*, *Breakheart Pass*, or as one of the *Magnificent Seven*. Extremely popular with his fans but not always with critics, Bronson once said, "We don't make movies for critics, since they don't pay to see them anyhow." To the left is the poster from Bronson's film *The Great Escape* (1963).

Steve McQueen (1930–1980), Class of 2014. The embodiment of cool, Steve McQueen will forever be remembered by Western fans for his starring role in the TV series *Wanted: Dead or Alive* and for films like *Nevada Smith* and *Tom Horn*. McQueen shined in iconic non-Western roles too, such as *The Blob*, *Bullitt*, *Papillon*, and *The Towering Inferno*. McQueen and fellow 2014 WOWS honoree Charles Bronson were two of *The Magnificent Seven*, and also appeared together in *The Great Escape*. At right, McQueen's son Chad holds up a sign at the 2010 dedication of Steve McQueen Square at the intersection of Highland Avenue and Santa Monica Boulevard in Hollywood. (Photograph by Kim Stephens.)

STEVE McQUEEN. Steve McQueen's skills as a motorcycle and race car driver were often put to use in his action roles. McQueen was no stranger to Santa Clarita, as he used to frequent the motocross track in Valencia in the 1970s. Today, McQueen holds a permanent place of honor on the Walk of Western Stars to commemorate his work in films, television, and on Broadway. McQueen is seen here in a still from *The Great Escape*.

Diamond Farnsworth (b. 1949), Class of 2015. Since the start of the Walk of Western Stars, Hollywood's unsung heroes—stunt performers—have earned their share of saddles on Main Street. In 2015, Diamond Farnsworth joined their ranks alongside such noted "fall guys" as Hal Needham, Loren Janes, Jack Lilley, Jack Williams, and his father, Richard Farnsworth. Over a 50-year career, Farnsworth doubled for several famous actors, including Sylvester Stallone, Lee Marvin, Jeff Bridges, Kevin Costner, Mark Harmon, and Scott Bakula. A few of the skills he brought to screen include race car driving and motorcycle riding, pistol and rifle marksmanship, rollerblading, surfing and swimming, ice skating and hockey, skateboarding, snow and water skiing, archery, precision boating, scuba diving, rappelling, wirework, and executing falls. Farnsworth has been the longtime stunt coordinator for the Santa Clarita production *NCIS*. He is pictured here surrounded by friends and family at the unveiling of his saddle in 2015.

Waddie Mitchell (b. 1950), Class of 2015. At the unveiling of his plaque on the Walk of Western Stars, cowboy poet Waddie Mitchell quipped, "Ya know, people have been walking over me for a lot of years now. This will ensure that they'll keep being able to after I'm gone!" The nickname "Waddie," which is a synonym for "cowboy," came from Mitchell's father, and before Mitchell was a poet, he was a true cowboy. Growing up on a ranch with no electricity, Mitchell learned to tell stories he heard from other cowboys. At age 16, he became a full-time wrangler and chuckwagon driver, and later trained horses for the US Army. All these experiences added to his collection of stories, which he learned to spin into rhyme and poetic meter in recordings, on television, and at festivals. Speaking of festivals, in 1984, Mitchell was one of the co-founders of the Elko Cowboy Poetry Gathering, which was the inspiration for the Cowboy Festival held every year in Newhall.

Hal Needham (1931–2013), Class of 2016. Hal Needham's skills as a stuntman led him behind the camera to the director's chair for several stunt-heavy movies, including the *Cannonball Run* and *Smokey and the Bandit* films, which starred Burt Reynolds. Needham not only performed breathtaking stunts, but also helped to invent devices that made the stunts possible. His work in the field elevated the profession for all stunt performers, and his efforts earned him a special Oscar, making him one of only two stuntmen—legendary Yakima Canutt being the other—to win Academy Awards. In addition to his saddle in Newhall, Needham has another interesting connection to the area. In the original *Star Trek* episode "Where No Man Has Gone Before," William Shatner shoots Newhall native Gary Lockwood, but it is actually Hal Needham who falls into the grave. Needham's grandson Mike is pictured at his grandfather's induction ceremony in 2016, surrounded by Santa Clarita City Council members.

Johnny Crawford (b. 1946), Class of 2016. Even as he aged into his 70s, Johnny Crawford's face never lost the boyish charm of *The Rifleman's* Mark McCain. Playing the son of rifleman Lucas McCain (Chuck Connors), Crawford provided an innocent eye through which the audience could experience the exploits of his father and the other denizens of the fictional town of North Fork, New Mexico. Millions of young boys grew up wanting to be Mark McCain, with a dad like Lucas McCain who could handle every problem, often with a few well-aimed shots from his lever-action repeating rifle. Crawford's career neither began nor ended as the son of the Rifleman. Before the show's run, he was one of Disney's original Mouseketeers. After it concluded, Crawford had a long career as a singer and as the bandleader of the 1920s-styled Johnny Crawford Orchestra. Crawford is an expert practitioner of trick roping, which he began when he learned a trick from Montie Montana on an episode of *The Rifleman*. Crawford displayed these skills on the rodeo circuit throughout the 1960s and 1970s. He is pictured at his WOWS induction ceremony in 2016.

Bo Hopkins (b. 1942), Class of 2017. Fans may recall Bo Hopkins from his roles as Clarence "Crazy" Lee in *The Wild Bunch*, as the intimidating leader of the Pharaohs in *American Graffiti*, or from over a hundred other roles in television and motion pictures. His life began in South Carolina, earning him a drawl that served him well in many later roles. Hopkins lost his father at age nine and joined the army at 16. Despite some rough times growing up, and a career often portraying bad guys, he has always been an approachable and affable friend to his many fans. Below, Hopkins is seen in a publicity photo from *American Graffiti* (1973).

Bo Hopkins as "Joe" Pharaohs in American Graffiti 1973

Andre (b. 1943) and Renaud Veluzat (b. 1946), Class of 2017. Newhall's Placerita Canyon has been the site of Western filming for over a century. During that time, several ranches in the canyon have been used for productions, including Fat Jones, Jauregui, Walker, Golden Oak, Sable, Rancho Deluxe, and the granddaddy of them all, Melody Ranch. Melody began a couple of miles south in the canyon and was the primary site for Monogram Studios' Western films. In 1935, owner Ernie Hickson lost his lease on the old property and relocated the studio to its present site. Gene Autry bought the property in 1952 and owned it for the next four decades. In 1991, Renaud and Andre Veluzat, a couple of affable brothers from Saugus who as kids used to peek through the fence to watch the filming at Melody, decided to buy the last remaining parcel of the studio, which included its original Western town. From left to right are Renaud, their father Paul, and Andre at the Western town at Melody Ranch.

Andre and Renaud Veluzat. In 1962, Melody Ranch burned down, and from then on, Gene Autry used the property as a retirement home for his horse Champion. After Champion died, Autry sold the 21-acre ranch to the Veluzat brothers, who used photographs from before the fire to painstakingly rebuild the lot's former Western town. Dozens of films and television shows have been made there since the Veluzats took over, including *Deadwood*, *Westworld*, *Django Unchained*, and *Once upon a Time in Hollywood*. The Veluzats own an additional movie ranch in Saugus, as well as a military movie vehicle rental company. Thanks to Renaud and Andre and their families, Newhall has remained a vital filming spot for Westerns to the current day. Co-author Kim Stephens is pictured above at the entrance to Melody Ranch in Newhall. Below is a set from the HBO series *Deadwood*.

JAMES DRURY (1934–2020), CLASS OF 2019. It is fitting that the actor who portrayed *The Virginian* on television would join the Walk of Western Stars in Newhall, since many versions of that classic story, including the first silent version from 1914, were shot in the valley. James Drury also appeared in many classic Western movies like *Ride the High Country* alongside Walk of Western Stars recipient Joel McCrea. When Drury was notified of his Walk of Western Stars award, he filmed a special thank-you message from his home in Texas, in which he said, "Westerns, by definition, are morality plays. They must show the triumph of good over evil, and I don't think you can over-emphasize that." Drury, who passed away the following year, was represented at the unveiling of his saddle by his son Timothy Drury.

Robert Fuller (b. 1933), Class of 2019. Before appearing in over 240 Western roles, Robert Fuller worked as a doorman at Grauman's Chinese Theater in Hollywood. He later became the assistant manager at the theater before becoming an extra. Eventually landing speaking roles, Fuller went on to play leads on the popular television series *Laramie* and *Wagon Train*, and as Dr. Kelly Brackett on the 1970s TV hit *Emergency!* He was represented by his son Patrick Fuller at his saddle's unveiling ceremony, who read a letter from his father that said, "I am deeply honored to have received this award and proud to be joining the many great Western stars who have already been honored with a plaque on the Walk of Western Stars." Fuller is pictured in a scene from the television Western *Wagon Train*.

Dan White (1908–1980), Class of 2019. Like his hero William S. Hart, who helped him get his start in the film business, Dan White lived in Hollywood and Newhall for most of his motion picture career and shot many of his movies and TV shows in the Santa Clarita Valley. White appeared in over 260 Western roles in such famous films as *The Yearling*, *Red River*, *Giant*, and *Duel in the Sun*. Classic film buffs may recognize him in *To Kill a Mockingbird*, *Jailhouse Rock*, and as the customs agent in the famously long tracking shot at the beginning of Orson Welles's *Touch of Evil*. Having passed away in 1980, White's award was accepted at the event by his grandson John F. White and other members of his family. At the ceremony, his grandson quoted White as often saying, "Being a character actor meant everybody knew who you were, but nobody knew your name."

Cesar Romero (1907–1994), Class of 2020. Western fans will remember him as cinema's *The Cisco Kid* and from several guest-starring roles on TV Westerns. But for those who owned a television in the 1960s, the Cesar Romero role they will remember is the Joker on TV's *Batman*. For many caped-crusader fans, Romero will always be the one-and-only Joker, despite many famous actors having tackled the demanding role since. Older fans and film-history buffs may remember Romero from the movies as a Latin lover, exotic distinguished gentleman, and accomplished dancer. Having worked for the studio system, he made a name for himself by playing several roles as the suave, cultured foreigner. An example is the Afghan warlord he played in the John Ford/Shirley Temple film *Wee Willie Winkie*. Romero's induction ceremony has been put on hold due to the coronavirus. Pictured is a publicity shot with Romero and Carole Landis from *A Gentleman at Heart* (1942).

Ricky Schroder (b. 1970), Class of 2020. Ricky Schroder has been a familiar face on American film and television screens since he was a child. He debuted as a nine-year-old in *The Champ* in a performance that earned him a Golden Globe award for Best New Male Star in a Motion Picture. During his teenage years, he starred for five seasons on the sitcom *Silver Spoons*. As an adult, Schroder has made several memorable screen appearances, most notably as Newt on the Western miniseries *Lonesome Dove* and as Danny Sorenson for three seasons on *NYPD Blue*. His plaque unveiling has been delayed by the covid-19 pandemic. Pictured here are Schroder (second from right) with, from left to right, Becca Johnson, co-author E.J. Stephens, Kit Johnson, co-author Kim Stephens, Bill Heller, and Debra Heller at the 2020 Newhallywood Silent Film Festival at William S. Hart Park.

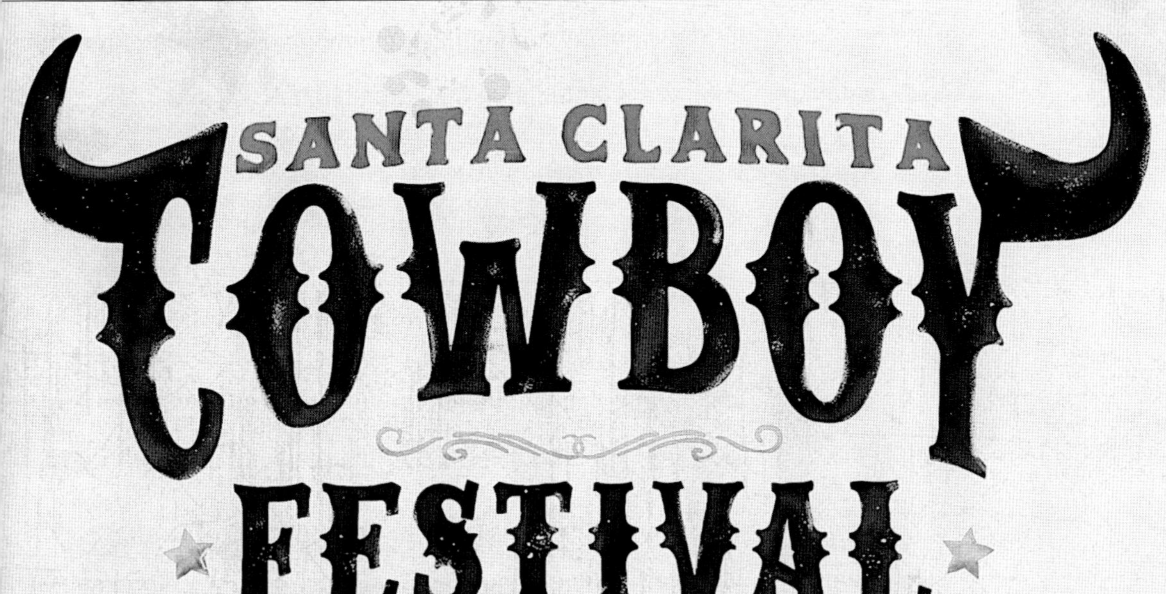

The Santa Clarita Cowboy Festival (founded 1994). Each April, over 10,000 Western fans from around the world make a pilgrimage to the William S. Hart Park in Newhall to experience a weekend in the Old West, with dozens of musical acts, dancers, poets, vendors, reenactors, authors, and lecturers. Guests can see demonstrations of trick roping and shooting, bull riding, life around the chuckwagon, a Civil War reenactment with Buffalo Soldiers, and a Plains Native American camp with tipis. During the weekend, visitors can explore the William S. Hart mansion and ranch house, experience the Saugus train station and train engine, the Historic Heritage Junction town, tour local Western film sites, and gorge themselves on the best peach cobbler west of the Pecos. The Santa Clarita Cowboy Festival began in 1994 as a way for Santa Clarita to share its 150-year Old West heritage with lovers of that colorful era. To learn more, visit CowboyFestival.org. By the way, there is another activity guests can experience for free at the festival: the unveiling of the saddles ceremony on Newhall's Walk of Western of Stars.